"AN HONORABLE PROFESSION"

"AN HONORABLE PROFESSION"
A TRIBUTE TO ROBERT F. KENNEDY

EDITED BY PIERRE SALINGER, EDWIN GUTHMAN,
FRANK MANKIEWICZ, AND JOHN SEIGENTHALER

DOUBLEDAY AND COMPANY, INC.　　　GARDEN CITY, NEW YORK

We wish to thank the following individuals and organizations, for permission to use the selections in this book:

Mr. Joseph Alsop, for his article, "The Kennedy Stumping Style"; Mr. Eugene Patterson, *The Atlantic Constitution*, for his editorial, "Robert Kennedy: The Children's Man"; Ambassadors James Bell and Averell Harriman, Representative Edith Green, and Senators Jacob Javits, Edward M. Kennedy, Winston L. Prouty, Abraham A. Ribicoff, and Joseph Tydings, for their eulogies; Steve Bell, for his commentary on ABC's *Perspective*, June 9, 1968; Bruce Biossat, for his article, "Kennedy, Man of Controversy: Warm, Tough, Loved, Feared" (Newspaper Enterprise Association); *Blackfoot News*, for "A Wake for Senator Kennedy"; Herbert L. Block, for his cartoon from *The Washington Post*, copyright © 1968 Herblock, *The Washington Post*; *The Boston Globe*, for "Robert Kennedy—He Understood Those Who Had Been Left Out" by Robert Healy; *The Boston Herald Traveler*, for an editorial, "The Only Way We Can Live" and for "Harvard Stadium Visit Recalls Kennedy the Athlete" by George Sullivan; Art Buchwald, for his piece, "Down the Rapids with Bob Kennedy"; James W. L. Park, Associate Warden, and the inmates, California State Prison at San Quentin, for the inmates' letter to Mrs. Kennedy, and for the Indian Prayer; *Chicago Sun-Times*, for "Poignant Lull in RFK Campaign" and "All Levels, All Colors—RFK's Kind of Crowd" by David Murray; Mrs. Gertrude Claflin, for her letter to Mrs. Kennedy; Thomas Congdon, Jr., *The Saturday Evening Post*, for his piece, "Kennedy Among the People," copyright © 1968 by Curtis Publishing Company; Mr. John Douglas, for his letter to Mrs. Kennedy; *El Malcriado*, for "Our Friend, May He Rest in Peace" by Antonio Orendain, translated from the Spanish; *Epoca*, for material from their special memorial edition; Mr. and Mrs. Thomas Germano, for Anthony Germano's letter to Mrs. Kennedy; Ambassador Arthur Goldberg and Secretary General U Thant, for their tributes to Robert F. Kennedy at Holy Family Church; The Hall Syndicate, Inc., for Charles Bartlett's column from the June 7, 1968, *New York Daily Column*, and for Joseph Kraft's "Kennedy's Oregon Defeat Tells Much of His Nature" from the May 30, 1968, *Los Angeles Times*; *Jet* magazine and Simeon Booker, for "Tickertape USA" by Simeon Booker; Kayham International, for "Blow to Humanity"; *Life*, for two articles by Loudon Wainwright, and for "The Wearing Last Weeks and a Precious Last Day"

Library of Congress Catalog Card Number 68-55381
Copyright © 1968 by Robert F. Kennedy Memorial Fund
All Rights Reserved
Printed in the United States of America

by Theodore H. White; *Look*, for pieces by Frank Mankiewicz and Charles Evers in *Look's* Memorial Edition and for the article by Warren Rogers and Stanley Tretick *RFK: The Bob Kennedy We Knew* from the July 9, 1968, issue of *Look*, all copyright © 1968 by Cowles Communications, Inc.; The Sterling Lord Agency, for "Kennedy's Arithmetic" by Jimmy Breslin; The Los Angeles Times Syndicate, for Hugh Haynie's cartoon, from the *Louisville Courier-Journal; Los Angeles Underground*, for "Not a Bad Dude" by James Thomas Jackson; Patrick J. Lucey, for his speech before the Wisconsin convention; Senator George McGovern, for his introduction at Sioux Falls; Harold Macmillan, for an interview on The British Broadcasting Corporation, June 7, 1968; Sylvan Meyer, *The Daily Times*, Gainesville, Georgia, for his article, "Kennedy, the Man, Widely Misunderstood"; W. F. Minor, *New Orleans Times-Picayune*, for his article, "Senator Kennedy in Mississippi"; Newhouse National News Service, for "The Other Side of Bob Kennedy" by Bonnie Angelo, and for "Kennedy in Defeat" by Jules Witcover; *New York Daily News*, for Ted Lewis's article, June 6, 1968; *The New York Times*, for "A Hushed City Says a Gentle Good-Bye" by Murray Schumach, and "Kennedy as a New Yorker" by Martin Arnold, both copyright © 1968 by The New York Times Company; *The New Yorker*, for material from "The Talk of the Town," June 15, 1968, copyright © 1968 by The New Yorker Magazine, Inc.; *Saturday Review* and the authors, for "The Meaning of Political Murder" by Charles Frankel, "RFK: A Personal Memoir" by Theodore Sorensen, and "Impressions at St. Patrick's" by Norman Cousins, all copyright © 1968 by Saturday Review, Inc.; Arthur Schlesinger, Jr., for "Kennedy's Stature More Than Legacy," *The Washington Post*, June 9, 1968; Prince Sihanouk of Cambodia, for his letter to Mrs. Kennedy; William Jay Smith and Nicholas Fersen, for their translation of Andrei Voznesensky's "June '68"; The Squire Newspapers, for "RFK a Week Later" by Tom Leathers; *The Village Voice*, for "The Stones at the Bottom of the Hill" by Jack Newfield, copyright © 1968 by The Village Voice, Inc.; *The Washington Post*, for their editorial, "A Gift of Courage," and for two articles by Richard Harwood, "The Old and New Kennedy Illusions" and "He Is the Most Compassionate of All the Kennedys"; Mr. James Whittaker, for his speech at the State Convention in Washington; and Miss Judy Zimmermann, for her letter to Mrs. Kennedy.

Doubleday and Company, Inc.
is proud to have played a part in the publication
of this memorial
to the late Senator Robert F. Kennedy,
a man who meant so much to his country.
We are grateful, too, in the knowledge
that the proceeds from the sale of this book
will be given over to the support of
the Robert F. Kennedy Memorial Fund.

Authorized by the Kennedy family.

The editors wish to express their appreciation and to thank those who gave so generously of their time in making this book possible. We are particularly indebted to Barbara Coleman, Pat Riley, and Gail Tirana who worked in Senator Robert Kennedy's campaign for the Presidency and who did such an effective and comprehensive job of research for this tribute. We also appreciate the help of Lisa Drew of Doubleday and Company who acted as a highly efficient liaison between the editors and the many persons whose words are reproduced here.

Doubleday and Company responded magnificently to our request that they print this book, despite the fact it is not a commercial venture and all profits go to a fund being created to carry on the ideals of Senator Robert Kennedy.

Finally, there is no real way we can thank Mrs. Ethel Kennedy and Senator Edward Kennedy for their support and their counsel.

PHOTO CREDITS

Page ix	Larry Schiller
Page 9	Look Magazine photo by Stanley Tretick
Page 22	Douglas Jones
Page 51	Paul Conklin—PIX
Page 53	Look Magazine photo by Stanley Tretick
Page 95	Bill Eppridge, Life Magazine © Time Inc.
Page 104	© The National Geographic Society
Page 120	Look Magazine photo by Stanley Tretick
Page 130	Burton Bernisky
Page 158	Look Magazine photo by Stanley Tretick
Page 172	Courtesy of Mrs. Robert F. Kennedy
Page 179	Steve Shapiro, Black Star

To Ethel

Challenge is the core and mainspring
of all human activity. If there's
an ocean, we cross it; if there's a
disease, we cure it; if there's a wrong
we right it; if there's a record, we
break it; and finally, if there's a
mountain, we climb it.

James Ramsey Ullman

An honorable profession calls forth
the chance for responsibility and
the opportunity for achievement;
against these measures politics is
a truly exciting adventure.

Senator Robert F. Kennedy

SENATOR EDWARD M. KENNEDY
EULOGY
June 8, 1968

On behalf of Mrs. Robert Kennedy, her children and the parents and sisters of Robert Kennedy, I want to express what we feel to those who mourn with us today in this cathedral and around the world.

We loved him as a brother and father and son. From his parents, and from his older brothers and sisters—Joe, Kathleen and Jack—he received inspiration which he passed on to all of us. He gave us strength in time of trouble, wisdom in time of uncertainty, and sharing in time of happiness. He was always by our side.

Love is not an easy feeling to put into words. Nor is loyalty, or trust or joy. But he was all of these. He loved life completely and lived it intensely.

A few years back, Robert Kennedy wrote some words about his own father and they expressed the way we in his family feel about him. He said of what his father meant to him:

"What it really all adds up to is love—not love as it is described with much facility in popular magazines, but the kind of love that is affection and respect, order, encouragement, and support. Our awareness of this was an incalculable source of strength, and because real love is something unselfish and involves sacrifice and giving, we could not help but profit from it."

"Beneath it all, he has tried to engender a social conscience. There were wrongs which needed attention. There were people who were poor and who needed help. And we have a responsibility to them and to this country. Through no virtues and accomplishments of our own, we have been fortunate enough to be born in the United States under the most comfortable conditions. We, therefore, have a responsibility to others who are less well off."

This is what Robert Kennedy was given. What he leaves us is what he said, what he did and what he stood for. A speech he made to the young people of South Africa on their Day of Affirmation in 1966 sums it up the best, and I would read it now:

"There is a discrimination in this world and slavery and slaughter and starvation. Governments repress their people; and millions are trapped in poverty while the nation, grows rich; and wealth is lavished on armaments everywhere.

"These are differing evils, but they are the common works of man. They reflect the imperfection of human justice, the inadequacy of human compassion, our lack of sensibility toward the sufferings of our fellows:

"But we can perhaps remember—even if only for a time—that those who live with us are our brothers, that they share with us the same short moment of life; that they seek—as we do—nothing but the chance to live out their lives in purpose and happiness, winning what satisfaction and fulfillment they can.

"Surely this bond of common faith, this bond of common goal, can begin to teach us something. Surely we can learn, at least, to look at those around us as fellow men. And surely we can begin to work a little harder to bind up the wounds among us and to become in our own hearts brothers and countrymen once again.

"Our answer is to rely on youth—not a time of life but a state of mind, a temper of the will, a quality of imagination, a predominance of courage over timidity, of the appetite for adventure over the love of ease. The cruelties and obstacles of this swiftly changing planet will not yield to obsolete dogmas and outworn slogans. They cannot be moved by those who cling to a present that is already dying, who prefer the illusion of security to the excitement and danger that comes with even the most peaceful progress. It is a revolutionary world we live in; and this generation at home and around the world, has had thrust upon it a greater burden of responsibility than any generation that has ever lived.

"Some believe there is nothing one man or one woman can do against the enormous array of the world's ills. Yet many of the world's great movements, of thought and action, have flowed from the work of a single man. A young monk began the Protestant Reformation, a young general extended an empire from Acedonia to the borders of the earth, and a young woman reclaimed the territory of France. It was a young Italian explorer who discovered the New World, and the thirty-two-year-old Thomas Jefferson who proclaimed that all men are created equal.

"These men moved the world, and so can we all. Few will have the greatness to bend history itself, but each of us can work to change a small portion of events, and in the total of all those acts will be written the history of this generation. It is from numberless diverse acts of courage and belief that human history is shaped. Each time a man stands up for an ideal, or acts to improve the lot of others, or strikes out against injustice, he sends forth a tiny ripple of hope, and crossing each other from a million different centers of energy and daring those ripples build a current that can sweep down the mightiest walls of oppression and resistance.

"Few are willing to brave the disapproval of their fellows, the censure of their colleagues, the wrath of their society. Moral courage is a rarer commodity than bravery in battle or great intelligence. Yet it is the one essential, vital quality for those who seek to change a world that yields most painfully to change. And I believe that in this generation those with the courage to enter the moral conflict will find themselves with companions in every corner of the globe.

"For the fortunate among us, there is the temptation to follow the easy and familiar paths of personal ambition and financial success so grandly spread before those who enjoy the privilege of education. But that is not the road history has marked out for us. Like it or not, we live in times of danger and uncertainty. But they are also more open to the creative energy of men than any other time in history. All of us will ultimately be judges and as the years pass we will surely judge ourselves on the effort we have contributed to building a new world society and the extent to which our ideals and goals have shaped that effort.

"The future does not belong to those who are content with today, apathetic toward common problems and their fellow man alike, timid and fearful in the face of new ideas and bold projects. Rather it will belong to those who can blend vision, reason and courage in a personal commitment to the ideals and great enterprises of American Society.

"Our future may lie beyond our vision, but is not completely beyond our control. It is the shaping impulse of America that neither fate nor nature nor the irresistible tides of history, but the work of our own hands, matched to reason and principle, will determine our destiny. There is pride in that, even arrogance, but there is also experience and truth. In any event, it is the only way we can live."

This is the way he lived. My brother need not be idealized, or enlarged in death beyond what he was in life, to be remembered simply as a good and decent man, who saw wrong and tried to right it, saw suffering and tried to heal it, saw war and tried to stop it.

Those of us who loved him and who take him to his rest today pray that what he was to us and what he wished for others will someday come to pass for all the world.

As he said many times, in many parts of this nation, to those he touched and who sought to touch him:

"Some men see things as they are and say why.

"I dream things that never were and say why not."

ROBERT F. KENNEDY
DEMOCRATIC NATIONAL CONVENTION
August 1964

Mr. Speaker, Mr. Chairman, Mrs. Johnson, Senator Jackson, ladies and gentlemen, I wish to speak just for a few moments.

I first want to thank all of you delegates to the Democratic National Convention and the supporters of the Democratic Party for all that you did for President John F. Kennedy.

I want to express my appreciation to you for the efforts that you made on his behalf at the Convention four years ago, the efforts that you made on his behalf for his election in November of 1960, and perhaps most importantly, the encouragement and the strength that you gave him after he was elected President of the United States.

I know that it was a source of the greatest strength to him to know that there were thousands of people all over the United States who were together with him, dedicated to certain principles and to certain details.

No matter what talent an individual possesses, what energy he might have, no matter how much integrity and how much honesty he might have, if he is by himself, and particularly a political figure, he can accomplish very little. But if he is sustained, as President Kennedy was, by the Democratic Party all over the United States, dedicated to the same things that he was attempting to accomplish, he can accomplish a great deal.

No one knew that more than President John F. Kennedy. He used to take great pride in telling of the trip that Thomas Jefferson and James Madison made up the Hudson River in 1800 on a botanical expedition searching for butterflies; that they ended up down in New York City and that they formed the Democratic Party.

He took great pride in the fact that the Democratic Party was the oldest political party in the world, and he knew that this linkage of Madison and Jefferson with the leaders in New York combined the North and South and combined the industrial areas of the country with the rural farms. This combination was always dedicated to progress and all of our Presidents have been dedicated to progress.

He thought of Thomas Jefferson and the Louisiana Purchase, and also when Jefferson realized that the United States could not remain on the Eastern Seaboard and sent Lewis and Clark to the West Coast; of Andrew Jackson; of Woodrow Wilson; of Franklin Roosevelt, who saved our citizens who were in great despair because of the financial crisis; of Harry Truman who not only spoke but acted for freedom.

So, when he became President he not only had his own principles and his own ideals but he had the strength of the Democratic Party. As President he wanted to do something for the mentally ill and the mentally retarded; for those who were not covered by Social Security; for those who were not receiving an adequate minimum wage; for those who did not have adequate housing; for our elderly people who had difficulty paying their medical bills; for our fellow citizens who are not white and who had difficulty living in this society. To all this he dedicated himself.

But he realized also that in order for us to make progress here at home we had to be strong overseas, that our military strength had to be strong. He said one time, "Only when our arms are sufficient, without doubt, can we be certain, without doubt, that they will never have to be employed." So when we had the crisis with the Soviet Union and the Communist Bloc in October of 1962, the Soviet Union withdrew their missiles and bombers from Cuba.

Even beyond that, his idea really was that this country, that this world, should be a better place when we turned it over to the next generation than when we inherited it from the last generation. That is why—with all of the other efforts that he made—the Test Ban Treaty, which was done with Averell Harriman, was so important to him.

And that's why he made such an effort and was committed to the young people not only of the United States but to the young people of the world. And in all of these efforts you were there—all of you.

When there were difficulties, you sustained him.

When there were periods of crisis, you stood beside him.

When there were periods of happiness, you laughed with him.

And when there were periods of sorrow, you comforted him.

I realize that as individuals we can't just look back, that we must look forward. When I think of President Kennedy, I think of what Shakespeare said in *Romeo and Juliet*:

"When he shall die take him and cut him out into stars and he shall make the face of heaven so fine that all the world will be in love with night and pay no worship to the garish sun."

I realize that as individuals, and even more important, as a political party and as a country, we can't just look to the past, we must look to the future.

So I join with you in realizing that what started four years ago—what everyone here started four years ago—that is to be sustained; that is to be continued.

The same effort and the same energy and the same dedication that was given to President John F. Kennedy must be given to President Lyndon Johnson and Hubert Humphrey.

If we make that evident, it will not only be for the benefit of the Democratic Party, but, far more important, it will be for the benefit of this whole country.

When we look at this film we must think that President Kennedy once said: "We have the capacity to make this the best generation in the history of mankind, or make it the last."

If we do our duty, if we meet our responsibilities and our obligations, not just as Democrats, but as American citizens in our local cities and towns and farms and our states and in the country as a whole, then this generation of Americans is going to be the best generation in the history of mankind.

He often quoted from Robert Frost—and said it applied to himself—but we could apply it to the Democratic Party and to all of us as individuals:

> "The woods are lovely, dark and deep.
> But I have promises to keep
> And miles to go before I sleep,
> And miles to go before I sleep."

STATEMENT BY SENATOR ROBERT F. KENNEDY
ON THE DEATH
OF THE REVEREND MARTIN LUTHER KING
RALLY IN INDIANAPOLIS, INDIANA—*April 4, 1968*

I have bad news for you, for all of our fellow citizens, and people who love peace all over the world, and that is that Martin Luther King was shot and killed tonight.

Martin Luther King dedicated his life to love and to justice for his fellow human beings, and he died because of that effort.

In this difficult day, in this difficult time for the United States, it is perhaps well to ask what kind of a nation we are and what direction we want to move in. For those of you who are black—considering the evidence there evidently is that there were white people who were responsible—you can be filled with bitterness, with hatred, and a desire for revenge. We can move in that direction as a country, in great polarization—black people among black, white people among white, filled with hatred toward one another.

Or we can make an effort, as Martin Luther King did, to understand and to comprehend, and to replace tnat violence, that stain of bloodshed that has spread across our land, with an effort to understand with compassion and love.

For those of you who are black and are tempted to be filled with hatred and distrust at the injustice of such an act, against all white people, I can only say that I feel in my own heart the same kind of feeling. I had a member of my family killed, but he was killed by a white man. But we have to make an effort in the United States, we have to make an effort to understand, to go beyond these rather difficult times.

My favorite poet was Aeschylus. He wrote: "In our sleep, pain which cannot forget falls drop by drop upon the heart until, in our own despair, against our will, comes wisdom through the awful grace of God."

What we need in the United States is not division; what we need in the United States is not hatred; what we need in the United States is not violence or lawlessness, but love and wisdom, and compassion toward one another, and a feeling of justice toward those who still suffer within our country, whether they be white or they be black.

So I shall ask you tonight to return home, to say a prayer for the family of Martin Luther King, that's true, but more importantly to say a prayer for our own country, which all of us love—a prayer for understanding and that compassion of which I spoke.

We can do well in this country. We will have difficult times. We've had difficult times in the past. We will have difficult times in the future. It is not the end of violence; it is not the end of lawlessness; it is not the end of disorder.

But the vast majority of white people and the vast majority of black people in this country want to live together, want to improve the quality of our life, and want justice for all human beings who abide in our land.

Let us dedicate ourselves to what the Greeks wrote so many years ago: to tame the savageness of man and to make gentle the life of this world. Let us dedicate ourselves to that, and say a prayer for our country and for our people.

JOHN GLENN
EULOGY

> The characteristic of heroism is its persistency. All men have wandering impulses, fits and starts of generosity. But when you have chosen your part, abide by it, and do not weakly try to reconcile yourself with the world. The heroic cannot be the common, nor the common the heroic. Yet we have the weakness to expect the sympathy of people in those actions whose excellence is that they outrun sympathy and appeal to a tardy justice. If you would serve your brother, because it is fit for you to serve him, do not take back your words when you find that prudent people do not commend you. Adhere to your own act, and congratulate yourself if you have done something strange and extravagant and broken the monotony of a decorous age. It was a high counsel that I once heard given to a young person, "Always do what you are afraid to do." —Ralph Waldo Emerson*

Perhaps Robert Kennedy saw much of himself in these words by Emerson. His life's commitment was indeed an "appeal to a tardy justice." He sought to dream possible dreams once thought impossible, and "to strive, to seek, to find, and not to yield," as Tennyson wrote.

He lived in a favored position, born to means but not demeaned by it. But in place of indolent leisure, he saw independence as a trust, a platform from which to rise, to act, to right injustice he saw in our midst. Above all he

*Underlined by Robert Kennedy in a book of poems and essays by Ralph Waldo Emerson.

was a compassionate man with deeply ingrained empathetic feelings and concern for those of lessened opportunity and hope.

In short, he cared—deeply, personally, and with a resolve for action. That we would rest while the American Dream was not a reality for every man was, for him,

"...just not acceptable,"
"We can do better."

In California, we had walked through a very poor area where several hundred people, mostly children, black, brown and white, surrounded Bob. The children ran, jumped, laughed, and sought his hand. He in return talked and joked with them as we walked through the midst of squalor—unpainted homes and unpaved streets.

Now, he stared out the window of the jet, introspective, lost in his thoughts, saying nothing, and hearing nothing of the typical campaign plane sounds. I sat in the empty seat beside him and remarked, "Something's really on your mind." He turned, did not say anything for a few seconds, then quietly replied, "Aw, I just keep thinking of those kids."

On the dedication page of his book *To Seek a Newer World* Bob started with a dedication, "... to my children and yours," followed by a quote of Albert Camus, one of his favorite authors.

> Perhaps we cannot prevent this world from being a world in which children are tortured. But we can reduce the number of tortured children. And if you don't help us, who else in the world can help us do this?

This concern for children was symbolic of the intense interest he took in all the molding influences that could shape the world of the future. As summarized in his announcement as a presidential candidate, he sought to work for the "reconciliation of men"—to bridge the chasms in our society between the races, between rich and poor, young and old, pro-war and anti-war, advantaged and disadvantaged, and between the nations of the world. This was a constant theme as he went to the people.

Within dissident groups he saw a uniting thread of similarity in their feeling of disengagement from the remainder of society; the feeling that "no one cares," that personal control over their own future had been lost, that nameless bureaucratic "theys" in a faraway, unknown office determine what will be, and that the individual is hopelessly and inextricably enmeshed in the system.

One of his purposes was to return authority and initiative to levels where we could heed Thomas Jefferson's words that each man must have his voice heard and considered in some council of government. In this lack, he saw a common ground of dissent shared by students, poor, Indian, and black that must be corrected. He was the champion of these groups because they knew he cared. He sought to learn of their problems. He went to campuses and heard student hopes and aspirations, to Indian reservations to see their homes and communities, to visit ghetto families, walking hand in hand with their children, letting himself be the "council of government" for all groups.

Bob was invited to attend a meeting with two hundred leaders of the black community in Oakland. Scheduling was a problem and we arrived after midnight at the end of a day of campaigning. At first, he was the only white person admitted to the meeting, but I was permitted to join him.

He listened while the Negro leadership poured out their spectrum of thoughts, complaints, suggestions, frustrations, and hates. From moderate leadership came constructive suggestions and plans. From extreme militants came a vitriolic torrent of threats and calls for armed action that were frightening in their implication. Many of our national leaders would not have been physically safe in that area and meeting, but Bob came to them, learned from them, and they from him, with mutual understanding and dignity.

With both groups at this meeting, and with all he met, Bob tried to reason, discuss, allay unjustified fears, counsel programs that would be practical and possible, unify instead of separate, and begin dialogues that would somehow bridge differences. He did not talk *to* a group or *at* a group, but *with* the group, a characteristic he displayed whether with students, civil rights leaders, poverty workers, or others representing major sectors in our society.

His interest and concern knew no national borders. Suffering, injustice, and deprivation were just as intolerable for him in other parts of the world. He felt mankind must somehow learn to live in freedom, sharing solutions to problems, or our difficulties would become insurmountable. As a nation favored beyond all others, we must and could lead the way.

No American felt and gave more pride, love, and dedication to his country —this "best hope for man"—than did Bob Kennedy. And the extent of this love and dedication made the inequities, the cancerous seeds of discontent in our midst, loom even more intolerable to him. The high calling of politics, the "business of all the people," was where Bob thought the most could be accomplished. So he ran for our highest office.

In a moving eulogy on the Senate floor, his New York colleague, Senator Javits, said in part

> His hope and idealism made him a force for constructive change which inspired the youth of the nation. He had, so far as I know, the deepest concern for the underdog of anyone I had ever met. To put it in very blunt terms, he had deep concern for the people whom our society—notwithstanding its many blessings, and it does have them —had disfranchised in terms of opportunity and in terms of the legacy to which we feel all Americans are entitled. He was not the only man in public life to have this feeling in his heart; but, in my judgment, it burned in him more brightly than in any other man I have ever known.

Beyond his public concerns, Bob Kennedy was also part of the same hopes, frustrations, loves, joys, sadnesses, frailties, strengths, and weaknesses that inhabit every man in varying quantities, and we should not deify him beyond reality. That would serve only to demean his memory. The stature reality gives him is enough. He will be remembered as many things to many people, as this book will bear witness.

He will be missed most by his family to whom he was a devoted husband and father. There was always time to hear a child's problem, give it serious thought and come to a mutually arrived at decision. There was a time to play, a time to share, and a time to be stern, for he was a father in the finest sense of the word. He encouraged the best in them, and they responded. The family was never far from thought, for his office was filled with pictures and mementos of special family occasions.

To describe the relationship between Bob and Ethel as one of love, devotion, and understanding, is only to admit the inadequacy of words.

To me he was a friend, with all that implies. Around a riverside campfire in Idaho the discussion turned from why I had named my spacecraft *Friendship Seven* to opinions of the components of real friendship. Bob then asked how many real friends each person thought they had, persons in whom complete trust could be placed. Some had trouble getting beyond the fingers of one hand. I can now count one less.

If there was a single personal charactistic that set him apart, it was an inordinate, probing, insatiable curiosity. He continually sought the why, the how, the reasons, and the motivations. A questioning nature, and wonder, are hallmarks of great men. These become a way of life which contribute not only a fund of knowledge and feeling, but also a pursuit of excellence, with constant questioning of whether we have done our best. "Wisdom begins in wonder," Socrates said.

Beyond the public stature and position of Bob Kennedy, there are a thousand cherished personal recollections that flood to memory. But evoking our memories of him in cold eulogy would be mockery if not followed by resolve to quicken the future he sought. Every American must be able to realize his full potential, unrestrained by race, creed, color, or lack of opportunity.

Bob Kennedy was cut short in years, so his full potential can never be known. But his vision, foresight, and dedication blazed paths that must eventually be followed to the heights. His role as catalyst in the mixture of our times will go far beyond his years. He saw hope where many could only foresee gloom. He was optimistic that man-made problems could also be man-solved. In unrest and dissidence, he saw not just problems but also the interest, energy, awareness, and activity that must be channeled to build solutions. To him times of change were also times of greatest opportunity.

> If there is any period one would desire to be born in, is it not the age of Revolution, when the old and the new stand side by side and admit of being compared; when the energies of all men are searched

"AN HONORABLE PROFESSION"

by fear and by hope; when the historic glories of the old can be compensated by the rich possibilities of the new era? This time, like all times, is a very good one, if we but know what to do with it.

—Ralph Waldo Emerson*

After several minute's thought, Bob Kennedy wrote an inscription in his book *To Seek a Newer World*. The book was for my son Dave.

> For Dave
> If we don't find
> it — you must —
>
> Bob Kennedy

Now—we must.

---

*Underlined by Robert Kennedy in a book of poems and essays by Ralph Waldo Emerson.

PIERRE SALINGER
TRIBUTE

I was riding in a small taxi down a country road in southern France last month. For a few moments now, the young taxi driver, his eyes intent on the road, had been talking of Robert Kennedy.

"In the village where I live, we were struck by his death as if he had been one of our kinsmen. There was sorrow everywhere." We drove on, and he was silent for a few moments. Then he added: "It was like killing El Greco or Rubens. Politics is an art, and he was an artist."

How few people talk about politics as an art today!

And yet, this French taxi driver who had never known Robert Kennedy was right. The politics of excellence and compassion and honesty is an art. And Robert Francis Kennedy was an artist.

He was the most unforgettable man I have met. Anything I am today, I owe to him. He had a superb gentleness and understanding. But the real joy of being his friend was that he always told you the truth. He did not try to hide his distaste for indolence and lack of purpose. He never asked a friend or an associate to do anything he would not do himself.

I knew Robert Kennedy for twelve years. You could not come into his orbit without being deeply affected. We were both very young when we met. It was a day in October in 1956, and I was a contributing editor of *Collier's* and went to interview him about his upcoming role as the chief counsel of a Senate Committee investigating racketeering in labor unions and management.

I came away from my meeting with mixed feelings. My interview was a total failure because the whole time I spent with this young man with those intense and piercing blue eyes was occupied in answering questions he posed to me. I also found him inordinately shy. And yet I left him that day feeling I had met an uncommon man.

That must explain why, barely ten weeks later when *Collier's* went out of business and Bob Kennedy telephoned me to ask if I would go to work for him, I agreed without a second's hesitation. It was a decision I never regretted for an instant.

Working for Robert Kennedy was not easy. In work as well as in play, he drove himself hard. An eighteen-hour day was commonplace. One night, he drove me home from the Senate at one A.M. after a day which had started at seven. As we swung out of the Senate Office Building, he noticed that the lights were still on in the office of Jimmy Hoffa in the Teamsters Building across the street. "If he's still working, we should be working," he said, and we went back to the office. After seven weeks of the grueling Hoffa hearings came to an end, we had a small party at my house for the members of the committee staff that went into the early hours. Bob and Ethel Kennedy were there. I could scarcely believe it when the phone rang by my bed at four o'clock the next morning and Bob suggested we go back to work. I do not want to make him sound like a martinet or a fanatic. He was neither. But he gave everything he had to anything in which he was involved. His enthusiasm was contagious.

In the twelve years which ensued I watched the development of a man into the ablest and most compassionate leader this country has ever developed. When I first met Bob he saw the world in rather simple black and white terms. His real growth was his ability to grasp the complexities of our modern world and to be able to understand the shades of gray which abound in the problems we face. He never compromised with principle, but the maturing Bob Kennedy was able to see and understand the adversary's position.

He had an inexhaustible curiosity about life that drove him in a never-ending search for more knowledge, for more understanding. You can tell almost as much about a man by the quality of his questions as by the quality of his responses.

One thing that never changed was his honesty. Sometimes it was almost painful to watch him answering questions from reporters. He seemed to hesitate—but what he was doing was rejecting the easy answer. It was because he was so honest that he was so believable. It was not an accident that the dispossessed of this nation loved and trusted Bob Kennedy. Time after time as Attorney General, as Senator, they tested his honesty and his commitment and found it genuine.

He could not stand the idea that other people suffered. When he talked of hunger and deprivation—he did not cite statistics—he talked in terms of the human beings he had seen. He wanted so much to ease suffering and injustice—he had such genuine compassion—that it almost became an obsession with him. The dispossessed understood that, and that's why they believed him.

There are a host of memories of this man which I cherish. When you worked for Bob you came not to expect those lavish words of praise for your efforts that employers sometimes bestow on their subjects. But the quiet words, expressed at the right time; the feeling that you had his confidence and that he trusted your judgment—these were rewards of far greater significance for those who worked for Bob Kennedy.

Four days after the assassination of President John Kennedy, I went with Bob to Hobe Sound. He was shattered by the death of his brother. At one point he organized a touch football game. I am not very athletic, but that game was as tough and vicious an encounter as I have ever been in—as if the brutal body contact would inflict pain to supersede the terrible pain we all felt at that time.

And then, there he was in my home in Los Angeles, getting ready for a man-killing day, playing with my two-year-old son with the affection of a man who loved children and in turn is loved by them.

This gentleness, this compassion, this honesty which I saw at close hand must have been communicated to that taxi driver in Southern France who had never met Bob Kennedy but who talked to me with such sensitivity and regret about his death.

As Robert Kennedy's funeral train wended its way south through the slums of Newark, Philadelphia, Wilmington, and Baltimore—through the beautiful open countryside of Pennsylvania and Maryland—all these thoughts welled up in my mind. But there was one thought which kept coming back as I looked at the people assembled on that train. The tribute to Robert Kennedy was not the quantity of the people on the train, but their quality. He had that remarkable ability to involve and to attract the best, the brightest, and most committed people. I doubt if Bob Kennedy ever called a single person in the top echelon of his campaign to ask them to come to work. They just came, giving up jobs and careers, changing their lives, because they believed in him. And so it was on the train. The passengers on that train could have run the most exciting government this nation has ever seen!

And that is why, while we weep for Bob Kennedy, we weep for ourselves and our country. I am so much richer for having known him; but we are all so much poorer for having lost him.

EDWIN O. GUTHMAN
August 14, 1968

It may be said in years to come that we who worked with Robert Kennedy were lucky to have had the experience. I believe that, but knowing Bob well makes his death so much harder to bear. It is in fact almost unbearable, for we were, as Bob put it, "a band of brothers," bound together by common purposes and indestructible friendships—and led by Bob.

There was about him a presence of command. Had he chosen a military career, he would have been the rare platoon leader or regimental commander whom men followed into battle believing that no harm could come to them as long as he was with them. But that was not what drew us to him. It was his deep commitment to do all he could to right the wrongs he saw and it was his constant concern for truth and justice. Finally, personal relationships were central to everything he did and he could inspire people to do extraordinary things by setting a high standard of courage and hard work himself and by giving loyalty to an exceptional degree. It is no exaggeration to say that there were many men who would have taken the assassin's bullet gladly, if they could have shielded their friend.

He did not make friends easily. It was necessary to go through some difficult experience with him—to test and be tested—but once formed the bond of friendship persisted regardless of the passage of time or a change of circumstances. Thus he would go to great lengths to help a friend or someone he respected, particularly if they were in trouble. To him that was the only manly thing to do, but in the twelve years I knew him, I heard him only once put it into words that revealed his innermost feelings. Oddly, but typically, it occurred in connection with Congressman Charles Buckley, a controversial New York political figure. In 1960 when John Kennedy ran for President, Buckley was one of four Democratic leaders who held 104½ votes of the New York delegation to the Democratic convention in Los Angeles for Kennedy—without which Kennedy probably would not have been nominated. To the Reform Democrats of New York and the New York *Times*, Buckley was the hated "boss of the Bronx." And they despised him. However, when Buckley ran for re-election in 1962, President Kennedy and Bob publicly supported him and Bob spoke at a testimonial dinner for Buckley in the Bronx in the spring of 1964. That fall when Bob ran for the Senate, he was asked repeatedly to explain how he could support a political boss like Buckley. Bob would reply that the Kennedys had gone to Buckley and asked for his support in 1960. "If he was good enough for us to ask for his help in

1960," Bob would say, "he was good enough to get our help in 1962 and 1964 when he needed it." At St. John Fisher College in Rochester, the familiar question about Buckley was asked and Bob gave his usual answer. Then he paused and looked up at the ceiling for a moment. "You know," he told the students, "that's the way relationships between men ought to be."

He was a wholly unique figure in our country. Never in all our history has a man been so close to the Presidency without actually holding the office. There was between John and Robert Kennedy an uncanny depth of understanding. It seemed as though one knew intuitively what the other was thinking. Bob was his brother's most trusted adviser and often his catalyst. He also was his brother's lightning rod. More than once when we suggested that he could legitimately beg off from some of the criticism that was directed at him, particularly in civil rights matters, he would say: "As long as it is on me and not my brother, that's the way I want it. I'm never going to run for public office." When destiny decreed that he run for office, he still met criticism head on. Political leaders and newsmen were repeatedly surprised at his effectiveness on the stump, not only how to handle tough questions but how to reach people.

It wasn't until he ran for the Presidency that many of them discovered that he had unusual rapport with young people, Negroes, and the disadvantaged. He didn't achieve this suddenly. It came because his willingness to face the hard truths about our society, his tireless sense of duty to the country and his compassion for people who needed help, had moved him to act where others made speeches and the Negroes, the young, and the poor sensed his honest concern. On March 5, 1961, six weeks after becoming attorney general, he spent the evening in Harlem, talking with the members of three street gangs. Their predicament—trapped in violence, poverty, and hopelessness—moved him deeply. That was the first of many such meetings he had while attorney general and senator, and out of it developed the President's Committee on Juvenile Delinquency and Youth Crime. The committee, prodded without fanfare by Bob, evolved the basic concept of the war on poverty—that each community mobilize its resources and develop its own programs for improving economic opportunity and education for the disadvantaged. His concern for the public schools in Washington, D.C., moved him not only to help in concrete ways—like repairing a high school swimming pool that had been closed for nine years, or finding jobs or raising money to enable students to remain in high school who would otherwise have dropped out because of economic pressure on their families—but also to visit the schools repeatedly just to show the young people that someone in high office cared about them.

When the white officials of Prince Edward County, Virginia, closed the public schools rather than accept court-ordered integration, the white children went to private schools, but about 1500 black children were simply cast adrift. It was intolerable to Bob and to President Kennedy that there were children in this country who did not have any opportunity to get an education. When all efforts failed to persuade the Prince Edward officials to reopen the schools, Bob acted. The Prince Edward County Free School came into being, drawing outstanding educators from around the country, and the Negro children received a better education than they could have ever hoped to have attained in rural Southside Virginia.

There was always a sense of achievement, purpose and excitement working with Bob. As he confronted a problem, his horizons widened and his understanding and maturity deepened. The young man who walked the streets of Harlem in March 1961, came gradually to understand the degree of frustration and hostility that was boiling up in the ghettoes. The first time he heard a young Negro say that he would not fight for the United States if it were attacked, Bob was deeply angered and the meeting broke up in a strong exchange of words. But Bob continued to meet with militant Negroes, to question and listen and see, and typically, he acted in a hundred ways to prevent the widening gap between the races.

One, his experimental community development corporation in the Bedford-Stuyvesant section of Brooklyn—the nation's second largest ghetto—bringing black leadership and white capital together to provide jobs and drastically improve living conditions, may, as John Goldman of the Los Angeles *Times* wrote, become his greatest living memorial.

"Some believe there is nothing one man or one woman can do against the enormous array of the world's ills," Bob said at the University of Natal in South Africa in 1966. "Yet many of the world's great movements of thought and action have flowed from the work of a single man. . . . Each time a man stands for an ideal, or acts to improve the lot of others, or strikes out against injustice, he sends forth a tiny ripple of hope. And cross each other from a million different centers of energy and daring, those ripples build a current that can sweep down the mightiest walls of oppression and resistance."

He was a man of his time, superbly equipped by experience, spirit, and judgment to lead, as his brother put it, the land he loved. He would have been a great President and that, plus the loss of his friendship, makes his death so difficult to accept, so unexplainable.

I hear him now saying, "That's not acceptable in this country. We can do better," or "Don't tell me what we can't do, tell me what we can do." And I remember so many things. I remember a night in May 1961 when the Freedom Riders were testing segregated bus depots in the South and a line of United States marshals held off a white mob that was threatening to burn a church in Montgomery, Alabama, where Dr. Martin Luther King and 1500 Negroes were meeting. At a crucial moment, Floyd Mann, chief of the Alabama State Police, led a detachment of troopers to the assistance of the marshals and subsequently the Alabama National Guard was sent in to prevent further violence. Governor John Patterson of Alabama was furious. He telephoned the Justice Department at 1:35 A.M., and berated Bob. The governor shouted that the protection the marshals had afforded the Freedom Riders was creating "a very serious political situation." When Bob was able to get a word in, he said in an even voice: "Now, John, don't tell me that. It's more important that these people survive than for us to survive politically."

Bob knew the odds on his survival when he decided to seek the Presidency. But after the Tet offensive had exposed the weakness of our military gamble in Vietnam and after President Johnson did not endorse the findings of his own Commission on Civil Disorders—much less move to implement any of the commission's recommendations, Bob was moved to risk everything in fighting for what he believed. It was more important that his principles and ideas survived than that he survived.

Now I believe the cause he carried to the country lives on; that he is with us and we are with him.

THE THREE KENNEDY BROTHERS AT PALM BEACH,
EASTER SUNDAY, 1957

FRANK MANKIEWICZ
LOOK SPECIAL EDITION

"The smooth-running, well-oiled Kennedy machine" got to be an office joke very quickly. Some forty people crowded into six rooms (five until early 1967) in the New Senate Office Building, handling 1000 pieces of mail a day, dealing with visitors, appointments, speeches, committee business, out-of-town appearances, and a daily average of seventy-five press queries—hardly a juggernaut.

As far as I was concerned, each day began with a race with Robert Kennedy to get the papers read. This meant the Washington *Post*, the New York *Times*, the New York *Daily News*, the *Wall Street Journal*. On Mondays, we added *Time*, *Newsweek*, *U.S. News & World Report* and *Life* and —every other week—*Look* and *The Saturday Evening Post*. There were more in the afternoon. I always lost. But when I caught up, we would talk, each morning, about which reporter had gained in perception (good story) and which had either not been listening or needed education (bad story). But he quickly forgot bad notices and remembered only genuine meanness.

Drew Pearson's nastiness was easy to explain, and so were the inevitably slanted New York *Times* editorials ("That's the *Times*—they just don't like Kennedys").

Once, last summer, the *Times* evidently thought for three Sundays in a row that what was "fit to print" was dashing pictures of Mayor John V. Lindsay on page one. When the third one appeared—a shot of the Mayor in sweat sox relaxing after a tennis match—Kennedy asked me: "What would happen if you called the *Times* and told them that next Thursday, I was going to play handball in the Senate gymnasium and would they send a photographer?" I tried that, and the *Times* was not amused.

The "ruthless" tag bothered me then, and it bothers me now. City halls, seats in Congress, and even a few statehouses are filled today by third-rate, cheap-shot politicians who have built small careers on tagging Robert Kennedy ruthless, but I never heard him attack any of them—or for that matter, anyone else in public life.

Still, there were the myths: He worked for the late Senator Joseph McCarthy with zeal, he somehow did unfair things to Jimmy Hoffa, he woke up the steel-price-controversy reporter at four A.M., he tapped people's phones and bugged their offices; he was, in short, ruthless and opportunistic. That none of these was a fact, that the truth of each could be readily ascertained at zero mattered not at all. People who would not believe the printed word when it went against their prejudices would believe almost anything bad about Robert Kennedy.

Why should this be so? It was, I think, for two reasons. One: He never ducked a question. I first met him at a State Department briefing just before his Latin-American trip late in 1965. He asked what he could say in Brazil, where the government had used Congress as a rubber stamp, outlawed political parties, jailed some opponents, banished others. A department official said, "Why don't you say . . ." and then launched into a masterful parody of diplomatic talk that added up to "No comment, but don't quote me." Senator Kennedy cut him off in the middle: "I don't talk that way." It was true. He had none of the politicians' small talk, none of that "Well, that's an interesting question. It seems to me that if you consider it carefully, it becomes a matter of. . . ." That sort of thing permits a man to use up fifty to a hundred words without saying anything, but without offending anyone or anything—except the truth. He would much more often answer "Yes," or "No," confounding the interviewer, who was probably counting on a rambling answer and hadn't yet thought of his next question.

The other reason, I think, is simpler. It was that people understood that he meant what he said. When he spoke of the "obscenity" of poverty or racial discrimination, when he said that the mistreatment of American Indian children, ripped from their homes at the age of five or six and taken to white men's boarding schools a thousand miles away, was "unacceptable," people sensed that he meant it, and meant to do something. If you shared his views, that made you more than a partisan. It led hundreds of grown men and women this spring to leave their offices, almost on an impulse, to help his campaign. If you didn't like his views, it led to a passionate dislike, and belief in every anti-Bobby story that came along. It was easier to talk about Jimmy Hoffa or the steel-price controversy than to face the reality that *President* Robert Kennedy might do more than talk about poverty, or the war in Vietnam, or the ghetto families and their children.

He was one of those rare men whose education continues after adulthood. He was learning all the time: from books, from his staff, his friends, the press, and from his joyous participation in the public life of his country. And, in the process, he taught us a lot. His analyses of men and events were as shrewd as his insights were illuminating, and the standards he set—for himself and his staff—had the curious result of making us all think we were better than we were.

The day after his funeral, a family left flowers at Arlington with the inscription, *"Escam dedit timantibus se"*—He nourished those who revered him. Also those who worked for him—and who loved him.

JOHN SEIGENTHALER
TRIBUTE

The early morning flight from Washington National Airport to LaGuardia was only half-filled with friends of Robert Kennedy who had come from St. Patrick's to Arlington to be with him for the last time.

Arlington now but a few hours behind them, they were bound back to New York, locked into an airplane for an hour flight to ruminate on the waves of anger, anxiety and frustration of the last few days which had run together in an unending stream of agony.

Some of the passengers, like Jimmy Breslin, the columnist, had known Robert Kennedy so well. Some, like an anonymous elderly black woman from Harlem, had never met Kennedy. But she loved him, too.

Two passengers were Japanese—one a substantial businessman, the other a young politician.

Tokusaburo Kosaka, the businessman, had been chairman of the committee which had welcomed Robert Kennedy to Japan during his visit in 1962.

Eiichi Nakao, now a freshman member of the lower house of the Diet, had served as executive secretary of that welcoming committee.

Nakao, who speaks English quite well, and Kosaka, who speaks it not so well, recognized a former member of the Kennedy staff as he boarded the plane.

His eyes suddenly full, Nakao leaped to his feet and embraced "the Kennedy man" he had not seen in six years.

"My friend," he said. "We are here with you. Mr. Kosaka and I are here to be with all the Kennedy people."

Kosaka's face, a mask of sadness, could not smile a greeting.

Nakao, as if he had come all the way from Tokyo in search of someone to tell his sorrow, let the words rush out in a flood. He and Mr. Kosaka had heard of the tragedy and had come at once. They had not made any advance plans; they had not contacted the Kennedy family or members of the Senator's staff. They had just come because they felt they belonged.

Somehow they had been admitted to St. Patrick's Cathedral for the funeral. They had not tried to board the funeral train. They had made their own plane reservations from New York to Washington and had waited five hours as the crowd grew at Arlington.

"I want to tell you," said Nakao. "I am now in the Japanese legislative branch. I was elected to what you would call your House of Representatives. I am there because I was inspired by Robert Kennedy.

"I watched Robert Kennedy when he came to our country. He gave hope to the Japanese young people. He debated with the Communist students and labor leaders. He was our hope. He was our hope."

The former Kennedy staff man thanked the Japanese friend of Kennedy—it seemed the thing to do—and walked on down the aisle of the airplane. He heard the elderly black woman from Harlem murmur to him:

"They think he belonged to them. We think he belonged to us. We think he was *ours*."

Robert Kennedy's former staff man—a white Southerner—had the distinct impression this unknown old lady had excluded him when she said Robert Kennedy was "ours."

He eased himself into the last seat in the cabin. Suddenly, down the aisle, roared Breslin, the burly, gruff newspaperman who was talking aloud to nobody and everybody:

"What a goddam, lousy shame," he said. "What a goddam lousy, filthy, wasteful shame."

And a dozen times during the hour-long flight he repeated himself.

There were, that day of the funeral and in the days that followed, glowing tributes to Robert Kennedy in the churches of America, in America's newspapers, in the halls of Congress and by commentators and celebrities on radio and television.

None were more heartfelt, and few were more eloquent than those expressed by a young Japanese legislator, an elderly black lady from Harlem, a tough newspaperman from New York.

Robert Kennedy made many trips to many parts of the world: to Poland and South Africa, and Indonesia and West Berlin and Latin America. Wherever he went he spoke the same language, with candor and passion. He welcomed debate, particularly from those who espoused the cause of Communism. He challenged the Communists to compete with the free, open society.

He had special words of hope for the young people of the world—tomorrow's leaders.

For them Eiichi Nakao spoke.

In the United States Robert Kennedy traveled to all sections pleading the cause of the disadvantaged, the poor and the forgotten citizens of this society. For them, the woman from Harlem spoke.

And Jimmy Breslin spoke for some of the rest of us.

THEODORE H. WHITE
LIFE MAGAZINE
June 21, 1968

All that week he had been tired. The deep tan, burned in by weeks of campaigning in the sun in the open car, lay over the exhaustion: the hair bleached blond, the fine fibers on the forearms almost flaxen. But he did not show the weariness except when you talked to him alone.

The Tuesday of the Oregon voting had been the worst day in weeks. He used the day to barnstorm through California's southland, from Los Angeles to Lakewood to Santa Barbara to Ventura to Oxnard to Los Angeles; and the crowds, as usual, were wild. They fed him the adrenalin to carry on; but in the plane, in conversation, the exhaustion was always there, under the determination.

He had few illusions. His last Oregon poll had shown him 30–29 over McCarthy, but the undecided vote was huge. And, usually, he knew, the undecided came down on the other side. He rambled on about Oregon, returning constantly to its beauties and the spectacle of its fir-covered slopes and green valleys. But it had been a cold state to him; Oregon, a great white suburb, had no problems; he knew he frightened Oregon by what he spoke of and his visions.

He talked: about the huge crowds in California and crowds as a serious index of response; about Vietnam—the negotiations should have begun much earlier, but he trusted Harriman to make the case. If we *did* have a case in Vietnam, this was the way to show it to the world—by talk, not by bombs. He felt we had already gained much in Paris by exposing the intransigeance of the enemy; but he was not hopeless of solutions—perhaps cantonment in South Vietnam, some new frame to give both sides in the fighting the security they needed.

Yet, always the conversation came back to the exercise in power which is a campaign for the Presidency. Oregon was lost, he already feared. So he *had* to make it big in California. Then, showing his strength in the most populous state in the Union, he might turn back East to deal with the local power-brokers. We haven't begun to fight that battle yet, he said. New York was uppermost in his mind. Unless he could show real muscle in California, his own faction-ridden state would be the arena of the most bruising clash this season.

People criticized him, he knew, for this extravagant spending of energy in the primaries. But, he kept saying, "Is there any other way of convincing them? Can you think of any other way?" If California went well, then he would rethink it, and might get those four or five days of rest before plunging into combat in New York. But now he was worn to the bone.

Then, that evening, winging north to Portland on a plane crowded with newsmen and cameras, with no crevice for privacy, the returns from Oregon had come in. Ethel gently held his hand, her fingers entwined through his or curled about his muscular wrist. He would not show his hurt; he smiled, talked to friends, strolled the aisle, encouraging the downcast, making clear he was going on with it.

The last week began badly, but he carried it off with courage, skill, and animal energy. When, on Sunday, California began to turn up—when he could sense, as a politician does, the return of enthusiasm in the surge of the crowds—he would not slacken his pace.

For he was an old-fashioned man of politics. And politics were people, a concept descended to him from his grandfather, who had known that truth three generations ago. He understood as well as any man the new technology of media and organization. His California campaign, pulled together finally, was running smoothly. The themes, pouring out of radio and television, were coming clear: an end to war in Vietnam; a new orientation for the federal government—which had come to him, after he could view the Executive from the outside, seeing government as cold, overcentralized, needing to be brought back to the people in their communities; and—a third theme—law-and-order, an end to violence.

Yet, the old politics meant this message had to be brought directly to people—by talking to them; had to reach their hearts and yearnings in person. Thus the last crescendo of barnstorming.

When he moved through a black district, or a Mexican-American district, the campaign reached a terrifying frenzy. It frightened one to drive in the open car with him—the screaming, the ecstasy, the hands grabbing, pulling, tearing, snatching him apart. To them he was The Liberator. In the other districts, always he pleaded—trying to explain America to Americans and show them the direction in which it must move. His staff insisted that he cool it; they, too, were frightened by the emotions he raised.

But he could not completely cool it. Briefed and briefed again on how to meet McCarthy in TV debate, he did so visibly with superb control. But though the voice and words were calm, his hands were moving, reaching, pleading.

Even when his polls in the final weekend turned upward, he kept at it until one or two every morning, then rose after five or six hours sleep, again to reach out, be with people. Until, finally, on Monday night, having barnstormed through San Francisco, Long Beach, the southland and reached San Diego, he collapsed. He could not finish the last speech; the enormous vitality had reached its end. He must rest.

Election day he slept late at the beach home of Evans and John Frankenheimer. Six of the children had been flown out to be with him, giving him the solace of a family day. Shortly after noon, he went out on the beach to frolic with them. It was no time for a solitary friend there to talk politics. So they kicked the rubbery, dark green kelp on the sand, and talked of the pollution of this beautiful coast and the disappearance of the great old kelp beds; they compared the Pacific to the Atlantic, and he preferred Cape Cod.

The sun would not break through, a chill mist hung heavy; but he stripped his flowered sunshirt and plunged in nonetheless. A huge roller came in and the bobbing heads of two children went under. Bobby dived; for a moment one could not see him in the surf, until he came up with David, whom he had pulled from an undertow. A large red bruise now marked his forehead. He had bumped either sand or the boy, but the boy was safe.

Now they came back up the beach to the pool, and children tumbled over him. Max, the three year old, wanted to walk the beach and bury coins in the sand. So they did. Then back to the pool, where Bobby tossed little ones through water, one to the other, as their glee rang out. Ethel, as tired as he, her hands placid in her lap, watched as he growled, teased them, let them roughhouse him.

Only once did he talk politics. He porpoised up, swam to the pool's edge and, with the inevitable curiosty of one politician about another, discussed his opponents' style and tactics—bitter about one of them, fond of the other. Yet, as always during these last few days, his conversation came back to New York, his home state, and how difficult it would be unless California turned out good, today.

It was not until after three in the afternoon that he received a private first flash. CBS had done some early sampling of voters as they left the polls and now guessed it might wind up as high as 49-41 Kennedy over McCarthy, with 10 for the Lynch-Humphrey slate. He sat there in the mist, in blue pullover and flowered beach trunks, and did not react to the news. Ethel asked whether it was good enough. He made no response. He wanted to know about South Dakota—were any early returns in yet? If South Dakota, rural, and California, the nation's most urban state, both went for Kennedy on the same day—then there was a real chance, not only in New York, but with the key brokers.

By now Richard Goodwin and Fred Dutton had joined him; they were pleased. Slowly the warmth and taste of victory came over him—and hope, too. He yawned, stretched his arms, suddenly drowsy, and said he thought he would take a nap. He left relaxed and confident.

It was the last time one would see him alone again. That evening in his huge suite, the rooms thronged with old friends, campaign workers, newsmen, there was no escape to share the joy privately with Ethel; friends and newsmen hunted them down from room to room as they tried to be alone for a moment, together. But the script of election night dictated otherwise. The votes were slow, but what was coming in was good and strong, a solid win, and the TV nets demanded their time. So he must wander from studio to studio to talk, answering again and again the old questions.

At midnight, ritual demanded that he go down to the screaming throng in the Embassy Room where, before the cameras of the nation and his supporters, he would accept victory. Then, after that, there would be a real party—Pierre and Nicole Salinger had invited the old friends to a celebration at their discothèque, The Factory. So they watched him go down the corridor, moving in a boiling mob through the entanglement of television cables—to the people, who were waiting downstairs.

The people. To him they were not numbers, nor digits, nor blank faces to be manipulated only by the new techniques. They were the very essence of politics. Impatiently, furiously, he had fought for them, and the passions he stirred were a response to the emotions inside himself, the deep feeling that the very purpose of government is to do things for people. For this, they called him "ruthless," an epithet that seared his spirit.

Once, overwhelmed by a Midwestern mob, he quipped: "All this for a *ruthless* man? Just think what they would do for a kind one." Although he joked about the word, it cramped his thoughts and public behavior.

Robert F. Kennedy wore his heart open at all times, and though strangers hated him with a venom almost irrational, it was what this impetuous heart dictated that they feared. All those who knew him best knew its kindness and courage, gallantry and tenderness. Its outer shell was the armor and lance he bore in public; and the style others hated was that of a man who jousted for the things he loved and never wavered in his faith.

There was no party at the end. His friends rushed to the hospital or to the hotel where the forlorn children slept. One could not explain this faith to the brave youngster, still awake, fighting back his tears at the horror he had seen on television. One could only hold the child, order hot chocolate for him, try to comfort him, fighting back one's own tears while recognizing the father's image in the good strong face of the child. And hope that he would keep the faith, as all his family had, in his country and people, hard now as it might be.

THE TALK OF THE TOWN
THE NEW YORKER
June 15, 1968

Shortly before five o'clock Friday morning, a gray light slipped into the city. The air was warm, the sky was hazy, and everything beneath seemed still. Two flags flanking the Fifth Avenue entrance to St. Patrick's Cathedral hung motionless at half-staff. On the south side of Fifty-first Street, a long line of people who had gathered during the dark of night emerged in ghostly fashion from the gloom of the cathedral's granite façade. Fatigue and sorrow could be seen on the faces. The line stretched back along Fifty-first Street to Park Avenue, and with the first glimmer of sunrise reflecting pink against the eastern sky it began to build, as, from all directions, and with almost no other sound than that of footsteps scraping softly upon pavement, the people of New York arrived to mourn the death of Robert Kennedy. Within a few minutes, the line doubled and redoubled itself until it reached Park Avenue, turned south, and began to fill up six-deep behind police barricades that had been set out on the sidewalks. Then, at five-thirty, the line began to move slowly toward the side entrance to the cathedral on Fifty-first Street near Fifth Avenue. People whose heads had been nodding in sleep awakened, straightened, and took stiff mechanical steps ahead. An elderly Negro woman who had been sitting in a folding chair got heavily to her feet and, assisted by a young man with shoulder-length hair, started forward with a halting gait. Behind her, a man in a wheelchair propelled himself as far as the steps to the entranceway, where two policemen came to his aid and lifted him inside. On the other side of the street, a busboy in a white mess jacket set on an ashcan before a restaurant and watched the mourners with tears screaming down his cheeks. Inside the cathedral, the line moved through the gloomy nave, down the long center aisle toward a maroon-draped catafalque that stood before the altar. The catafalque bore a plain mahogany casket that was flanked by six tall candelabras with amber tapers, and by six men who hd been close to Robert Kennedy, who formed an honor guard. During the night, television crewmen had erected several large scaffolds for their equipment, and a battery of powerful floodlights illuminated the bier with a harsh and unreal glare. The mourners approached the catafalque two by two and then separated to pass it on either side. Some people crossed themselves as they went by the coffin; others reached out and touched its lid; a few bent down to brush it with their lips. At six o'clock, a priest in red vestments began to intone the words of the Mass, and many of the mourners took seats in the pews and stayed on to listen and to pray. Very few appeared to notice that Edward Kennedy, who had stayed near the bier of his brother throughout the night, was sitting on the aisle in the eleventh row, looking straight ahead. Half blinded as they emerged from the darkness of the nave and into the merciless brilliance of the television lights, the mourners seemed to pass numbly through a corridor of total exposure. They included—white and black—nuns, girls in slacks and miniskirts, workmen in shirtsleeves, matrons and children, and businessmen wearing three-button suits and carrying briefcases. The words of the priest continued to echo through the vast cathedral: "Lord have mercy, Christ have mercy, Lord have mercy..." At quarter to seven, Edward Kennedy stood, drew himself erect, and, as if relinquishing himself to a river, joined the line of mourners, walking slowly into the searing light, looking at the casket containing the body of his brother. Then, following the others, he walked through the south transept of the cathedral and out to Fiftieth Street, where, in the rising sun, the tall buildings, trees, awnings, and other gnomons of this perpendicular city were beginning to cast the shadows that would mark the passage of the day.

It was seven years ago this month that we first saw Robert Kennedy close up, to talk to, and travel with around New York. In the last few years, and especially in recent months, he often moved in a hostile landscape; "Bobby," he was called by those who didn't know him, and some of them said it with contempt. We occasionally experienced a shock when we encountered the man himself. Lindsay always turned out to be Lindsay, Rockefeller turned out to be Rockefeller, McCarthy turned out to be McCarthy, but Kennedy bore little resemblance to most of what we read or heard about him. He was not "Bobby." We used to see him from time to time, and then, in March, we began to follow him quite closely—to California, to Washington, to Indiana, back to New York. He was, of course, an extraordinary man, a complex one; each time we saw him there was more to see. He could never be accurately measured, especially in terms of the past; he was always in the process of becoming. He was responsive to change, and changed himself. These changes were always attributed to his driving desire to win—except by those who knew him, who were aware of his great capacity for growth, his dedication, the widening of his concern. The people around him, we found, adored him—there is no other word. They would do anything for him, go any distance—and part of it was because they were convinced he would do the same for them. We, too, grew very fond of him. Beyond his associates and friends, however, was the public, part of which mistrusted him; he could not make a move without having his motives questioned. Some weeks ago, Joseph Alsop, an old friend of his, said to us, "So many people have him absolutely wrong. They think he is cold, calculating, ruthless. Actually, he is hot-blooded, romantic, compassionate." He was at once aggressive and reserved—a combination that was bound to lead to misunderstanding. And in Kennedy there was another rare juxtaposition of qualities: sensitivity and imagination together with a strong drive to accomplish things. He was both the reflective, perceptive man and the doer.

A TRIBUTE TO ROBERT F. KENNEDY

While we were on a ride with Robert Kennedy a couple of months ago, we made some notes. The night before, President Johnson had announced he would not run. There was a press conference in the morning, a lunch with a newspaper publisher, and then Kennedy got into his car to go to the Granada Hotel in downtown Brooklyn, where a hundred-million-dollar mortgage pool was to be announced for residents of Bedford-Stuyvesant. (He had worked hard on Bedford-Stuyvesant; one of his major projects had been to change that community, to save it.) Our notes read:

"On leaving the restaurant, Kennedy had a cigar in his hand. He still has it, but as he goes across town he rarely puffs it; it's just there. Kennedy scans the front sections of several magazines and the New York *Post*, turns and exchanges a few remarks, laughs, turns back, and then stares ahead, silent. When a traffic light changes to green, Kennedy's fingers twitch an instant before Frank Bilotti can accelerate the car. Bill Barry's eyes close; he is exhausted. He dozes. Kennedy was up until three o'clock. Carter Burden asks, 'Are you tired?' Kennedy shakes his head, murmurs no, no—brushing it off as if the question is not worth consideration. On the East River Drive, a taxi driver recognizes Kennedy and yells, 'Give it to 'em, Bobby!' Kennedy waves, then stares ahead again. He is deeply preoccupied now, at his most private. (When Barry wakes and offers everyone chewing gum, Kennedy does not hear him.) He abandons, piece by piece, the outside world—he puts away the magazines, the cigar is forgotten, the offer of gum is unheard, and he is utterly alone. His silence is not passive; it is intense. His face, close up, is structurally hard: there is no waste, nothing left over and not put to use; everything has been enlisted in the cause, whatever it may be. His features look dug out, jammed together, scraped away. There is an impression of almost too much going on in too many directions in too little space: the nose hooks outward, the teeth protrude, the lower lip sticks forward, the hair hangs down, the ears go up and out, the chin juts, the eyelids push down, slanting toward the cheekbones, almost covering the eyes (a surprising blue). His expression is tough, but the toughness seems largely directed toward himself, inward—a contempt for self-indulgence, for weakness. The sadness in his face, by the same token, is not sentimental sadness, which would imply self-pity, but rather, at some level, a resident, melancholy bleakness. For a public figure, Kennedy is a remarkably contained and solitary person, somewhat hesitant with intruders and, according to those who feel they know him well, shy. Silence appears to be his natural habitat. But he will suddenly break out of himself, and then he is very responsive—quick to laugh; funny in a spontaneous, understated way; generous to people who don't 'matter'; considerate, sensitive to others, and direct. He is unusually direct, in both good ways and bad—directness can be a major defect for a politician. Artificial situations make him uncomfortable; he is poor at masking his reactions. He does not indulge in much public self-analysis or explanation; he is inclined to keep quiet until he has made up his mind. This makes him appear cautious, or even devious—and makes his actions, when he does move, seem at times abrupt, 'political,' or contradictory. Missing from his make-up is the bland protective coloration of a popular politician; when Kennedy feels something, he is apt to speak out—or to remain totally silent, looking somber or glum—rather than to display indifference or gloss it over with pleasing chatter. There is not much change in the way he talks to one person or to a thousand, except for the formality. When he speaks of right and wrong, in either setting, he does not shift gears."

We watched him campaign. His energy was limitless. A day of relentless travel by car and plane, speeches, rallies, interviews might end toward midnight, when he and Mrs. Kennedy would stand on a high-school auditorium stage and shake hands with three or four thousands people. (Mrs. Kennedy's stamina, cheerfulness, and quiet patience, under difficult circumstances, were extraordinary.) Then, the next day, more of the same. He was, after each primary, exhausted—but he barely paused. Time was always against him. We saw him at his apartment the day he returned from Indiana:

"Kennedy spoke to his prospective New York State delegates in a restaurant early in the afternoon, giving an informal account of what he felt had been accomplished in Indiana and promising an intensive campaign in New York prior to the June 18 primary. Then he met with New York political leaders and others in his apartment. The apartment is still full of people: Ted Sorenson is writing in a back bedroom; another bedroom holds a small gathering; others are in the living room, others in the kitchen. Kennedy moves from one room to another, then sits for a moment in the hall as people stream back and forth past him. He is deeply worn, but nearly a month of intensive campaigning still lies ahead—Nebraska next week, then Oregon, then South Dakota and California. He rubs his face. He has pushed himself to the limit, but he does not mention his weariness. His face is gaunt, weathered; his eyes are sunken and red. He rubs his hand over his face again, as if to tear away the exhaustion. It is not something he has sympathy with, his hand is not consoling as it drags across his face—he is simply trying to get rid of an encumbrance. He responds slowly, haltingly, trying to think; the questions seem to goad him painfully to one more effort. In the wake of his success, he admits there are great areas of loss—primarily for his family, and in his privacy. 'I think . . . I think . . . I would make this one effort . . . and if it fails I would go back to my children. . . . If you bring children into the world, you should stay with them, see them through. . . .' He had once thought of teaching, or of starting a new kind of project in the Mississippi Delta, or of working with the Indians, but now he doesn't know. 'I think about it,' he says slowly. 'I think about it . . . I'm not sure.' The hand drags across the face again, his eyes closed. He mentions privacy. 'It would be nice taking a walk sometime without someone taking a picture of you taking a walk. . . .' More people come through the door. Kennedy looks up, gets quickly to his feet, and greets them, alert again, moving."

We remember an April afternoon at Hickory Hill, in McLean, Virginia, just before Indiana. He had come home for a few hours with his family. He sat in the dining room, eating a sandwich and discussing the farm problems of

Indiana with an agricultural expert. A small child sat at the table with him, gazing silently at his father as the talk revolved around hog prices. Other children flowed through the dining room, and each time one came past he would reach out—still listening, not taking his eyes from the expert—and hold, for a moment, his or her hand. After lunch, he played with each child. There was a gentleness in him, a capacity for love, that was not ordinarily revealed in print or in the pictures people saw of him. "Let us dedicate ourselves to what the Greeks wrote so many years ago," he told a group of Negroes in a parking lot in Indianapolis on the cold, bitter night Martin Luther King was slain. "To tame the savageness of man and make gentle the life of the world."

The world he lived in was changing fast; the past was less than useless as a guide—it was an obstacle. A man was needed who instinctively responded to what was real—a truly compassionate man with a sympathy for people and for people's need for change. As he walked, his head was always bent forward; everything for him was ahead. Now he is dead, and we see the films, over and over: he lies on the floor, his head cupped in the hands of others. He will no longer bring to bear on those forces he took such care to understand—the angry, divisive forces of our time—his vitality, his sympathy, his warm concern. His death is, in a word he used so often, unacceptable.

© 1968 The New Yorker Magazine, Inc.

LOUDON WAINWRIGHT
LIFE MAGAZINE
June 21, 1968

For those who had cared for him and watched him closely in these past hectic weeks, Robert Kennedy's going totally disjoints the sense of time. There he was, a moment ago, walking alone with the dog in a patch of grass in Oakland while the motorcade waited, and now he is dead, and there seems no possible way to link the two things together in the same chain of events. There he was, crossing a Portland hotel room on the night of his defeat in Oregon to shake hands with a friend, and now the campaign is a crushed, beribboned hat thrown in a corner of the Los Angeles ballroom where he joked, moments before he was shot, about his last victory. There he was, his blue shirtsleeves rolled up, walking and softly talking his way down the aisle of a plane bound for San Francisco, but suddenly there was a mass of screaming men and women in a passageway spattered with blood, and finally there was the hospital, its heavy stone face taking shape in the sunless dawn. The truth of death is belied by echoes of life which bounce around the chambers of the mind and dizzy the listener with false hope. Kennedy, moving his very fastest in a race he had entered too late, was dropped in midstride, and the watchers keep searching futilely ahead for quite another sort of finish.

The possibility of violence and danger was very much in the minds of the people who accompanied Robert Kennedy in his campaign. Surely the memory of his brother's death had something to do with it, and sudden recollections of that awful moment from the past were revived by fragments of sight and sound from the present. In April, in Logansport, Ind., the campaign party was chilled by the view of armed police standing on rooftops overlooking the block where Kennedy was speaking. "He's our guest," an official told me. "There haven't been any threats, but we just want to make sure he leaves town the same way he came in." Outside Gary in May the open convertible in which Kennedy and his wife were riding suddenly pulled off the road and people in the press buses gasped at the sight of the figures crouching over in the back seat. As it turned out, the stop had been made because Ethel Kennedy had got cold and needed to put on a coat. In San Francisco's Chinatown on the last day of the California campaign, virtually the whole party flinched at the sound of exploding firecrackers and there were other bad moments with balloons. People were frightened for him and kept saying so to each other; and Bill Barry, the devoted and powerful ex-FBI agent who guided Kennedy through crowds and clutched his waist as he stood up in the cars, often fell instantly into exhausted sleep in the airplane as we hopped from one tumultuous motorcade to another.

A TRIBUTE TO ROBERT F. KENNEDY

And of course Robert Kennedy deliberately and repeatedly exposed himself to the bad possibility. It was not that he sought the danger; rather it was that he seemed very much to need the actual physical contact with great masses of people. In crowds where people did not always reach up to grab or strike his hand, he reached out for theirs. It was quite literally a giving of himself, as if that were the best way he could renew the pledges he was making in speeches. Surely there has never been anything like this frenzied exchange of love in the history of American politics. And the prospects for trouble, accidentally or deliberately produced, were everywhere. He definitely did not want to be protected. And it was in a ludicrously insecure place—a narrow and jammed space which virtually any determined man could enter with a minimum of difficulty—where he suddenly needed it most desperately.

On the final day of the California campaign, Senator Kennedy invited me to ride in his convertible when he toured some of the poorer areas of Los Angeles, including the Watts district. The crowds that day were not as large as they had been on other occasions; still, people surged along the sides of the car in great waves, and it sometimes took three men—Barry, the Olympic decathlon champion, Rafer Johnson, and the huge football player, Roosevelt Grier—to hold Kennedy in his position as he stood on the trunk. Out of one crowd a fierce-looking and quite drunken young man with a goatee suddenly flung himself on the hood of the car and, sprawling there with his back against the windshield, began screaming at the people to "Make way for Kenne—dee! Make way for Kenne—dee!," and they did as he directed. The smack of hands against Kennedy's was constant, and his body shook under the impacts. When we got through one crowd and picked up speed to travel to the next place, the candidate climbed down into the back seat and his face was totally without expression. The eyes unmoving and distant, the whole look of him battered and stunned. Then he began to whisper into the ear of a pretty black child of about five or six who had somehow been put in the car and was now seated entirely happily between Kennedy's knees and, surrounded by huge strangers, was playing with a big white stuffed rabbit. The child knew her phone number and when we stopped a few moments later, Robert Kennedy gave her a hug and directed one of his workers to drive her home. Then he rose and got ready to meet the new crowd that was now moving toward him.

Outside the hospital in Los Angeles, a few hours after the shooting, the enormity of the tragedy began to settle in the minds of the weary men and women waiting in the street. Though some hope was held out, no one really had much. A woman reporter wept as she told of an invitation to a party Kennedy had planned that night. Somebody mentioned a train trip we had taken through Indiana and a joking song the press had written to tease the candidate. He had laughed at "The Ruthless Cannonball," and it was very hard to think about that good face moving in a laugh. In fact, it was hard to think that early morning, as it will be for many people for a long time, of that graceful man so mortally hurt. His campaign was over, and because of the quality of Robert Kennedy and the quality he wanted of his country, he had made it a tremendously promising one. From their headquarters, across town, several McCarthy supporters came and they looked absolutely stricken under the glare of the television lights. "Why did they shoot Robert Kennedy?" one of them asked. Another replied: "They shoot stars," and there can be no doubt that a real one came down that night.

DAVID MURRAY
THE CHICAGO SUN-TIMES
June 8, 1968

This was Robert F. Kennedy's kind of crowd, the hundreds of thousands who waited Friday in the sweltering heat for up to seven or eight hours, to pass, for just a moment, by the place where he lay, saying his own silent farewell to the people of the state he had adopted.

They were black and white and rich and poor and fit all those neat little cliché-type descriptive words used to describe crowds like those that were at St. Patrick's.

But they were more than that, too.

The other night—was it only a week ago?—after Senator Kennedy had lost the Oregon primary, his press secretary, Frank Mankiewicz, said in Los Angeles that the campaign schedule for California would be turned around and that "I think we'll go to our strength."

He meant going to the people who had flocked about Senator Kennedy in his brief, fiery political career, who had ripped out his cuff links and jammed every place he went.

They came by the coffin Friday, where the old friends and the dignitaries stood in silent vigil, to lay their fingers on the flag that covered the coffin, to stoop hurriedly to kiss it, or even, sometimes, to touch and then kiss their fingers—sort of blowing a kiss in reverse.

"Is that Martin Luther King?" one small Negro boy asked his mother.

And when they had passed by, they swerved back, many of them, for a final look and when they did, that was the moment to break, to place the handkerchief over the face and to sob. Or perhaps to have the tears come leaping into the eyes. And that was part of the strength of Robert Kennedy.

"Jesus, oh, Jesus," said one young, well-dressed woman, in a tone that suggested a benison for rather than blasphemy.

Then, they left, most of them, through the great door of the south transept, out into the heat and the barriers and the policemen saying, "Keep it moving, keep it moving."

Sometimes they would stop and walk into the south chapel and light a candle and pray silently, their eyes fixed on the statue of the Virgin above their heads.

One young girl, a picture of Senator Kennedy torn from a newspaper clutched in her hand, bowed her head and wept great tears, the sobs shaking her hunched body.

"This country stinks," said a youth in a black sport shirt. "Why do they have to kill a guy like this? He was trying to help everybody."

A lot of them wore Kennedy campaign buttons, as if to say that he may no longer be alive, but he was still their choice for President.

"We drove from Washington this morning and got here at ten o'clock," said a dark-haired, pretty young girl who had been working in the Senator's national campaign headquarters.

"There were four of us. We've been waiting seven hours. We probably could have gotten in some other way, but we didn't want to bother anyone."

There were the old, New York political friends, too, the kind of men with whom Senator Kennedy liked to sit around smoking one of his long cigars and talking about nuts-and-bolts politics, the glue that holds a political dream together and makes it strong.

There was, for example, Stanley Steingut, the Brooklyn Democrat chairman who was one of the first to champion the young man's cause because he saw a winner there. Friday, he stood outside the church, his face blank with shock.

Standing alongside the church in the shade was Paul O'Dwyer, talking to some people. O'Dwyer is an active reform Democrat here, a former city councilman and champion of causes, most of them lost, because those, he feels, are the only ones worth fighting for, like civil rights cases in Mississippi.

At a moment like this, when one talks to O'Dwyer, one gets the feeling that perhaps the country isn't going down the drain after all.

What brings all these people here, O'Dwyer was asked, as a young woman burst into hysterical wails and had to be led to a chair specifically placed outside the church for that purpose. What makes them react like that?

"It's the theater of it," O'Dwyer said, his voice rich with the accents of his native Ireland. "The theatrical quality keeps them from worrying about how miserable they feel."

Then he turned to someone else and started talking about the old days in New York politics, and other funerals and wakes, and it suddenly struck one how much, really, these no-longer-young Irish politicians had in common with the man they had come here to honor.

They and Senator Kennedy loved the power and the organization and the people they got to know, and they liked to get together and sit down over a drink and discuss whatever it was they were doing—in an election or in an organization.

And now the only man they have left of the Kennedys is Edward, and he's the Senator from Massachusetts.

But you have to like him, too, because he got out there Friday and walked along the sidewalks with only a couple of people near him, less than three days after his brother had been shot down.

And he seemed to be saying: "I'm a Kennedy and I don't believe in a world where a Senator or a presidential candidate or anyone else has to wall himself away from the people he is supposed to be leading."

"Was it worth it, waiting in line for six hours?" one older woman said. "For him it was. He was a good man. I wouldn't stand here like this—my feet are about to drop off—for anyone else."

So they waited silently, the important ones for a few minutes, the others for hours at a time for a brief walk by a flag-draped coffin placed under the lights. And then they turned and walked out the door, into the real world again, to try to make some sense out of the future. By the door was a collection box on the wall with a sign on it which said: "For the poor."

For the poor in spirit, presumably.

THE HANDS STILL REACH OUT

MURRAY SCHUMACH
THE NEW YORK TIMES
June 9, 1968

It was a gentle throng that extended New York's goodby yesterday to Senator Robert F. Kennedy, as his body was taken from the funeral service in St. Patrick's Cathedral to Pennsylvania Station for the last trip to Washington.

Across the street from the cathedral women, some holding rosary beads, wept softly. Many others raised hands to their wet cheeks. Some just waved limp farewells as the gray hearse passed down Fifth Avenue between buildings with flags at half-staff.

Men frequently put on sunglasses to hide tears and a number among the tens of thousands behind barricades guarded by the police looked down as though in silent prayer. Many aimed cameras with misty eyes.

There was very little hysteria despite the heat and dense crowds, particularly near the cathedral.

Fairly typical of the emotion and sense of private grief that pervaded this crowd, often eight deep, was the reaction when the cathedral loud-speakers carried "The Battle Hymn of the Republic" across the hushed streets.

As the choir inside the church sang the refrain of "Glory, glory Hallelujah," it was taken up by a small group of Negro men and women at the northeast corner of Fiftieth Street and Fifth Avenue. At first their voices were just a murmur. But as the last chorus began, a middle-aged woman's voice gathered strength and carried with rich fervor, causing many others in the crowd to join, while many wept.

But the full depth of mourning for the crowd began at 10:22, when the gray hearse glided up to the massive bronze doors of the cathedral as the loudspeaker brought to the solemn spectators:

"And they shall be with the Lord forever."

Almost without realizing it, the crowd began pressing forward. At times between pleas by the police to move back, men and women said, "Sh, sh," as though fearful the occasion might be marred.

Once the hush in the crowd across the street from the cathedral was so complete that the flap of a pigeon's wings was audible for almost half a block.

The climax came as the flag-draped coffin was borne down the cathedral steps and placed in the hearse. Then the sobs spread and a few women became hysterical. One was guided to an ambulance.

As the hearse started down Fifth Avenue, accompanied by a murmur of weeping as it passed, the police found it unnecessary to control the crowd. It spilled over into the crossstreets and cars made no effort to move.

At Forty-second Street an extraordinary thing occurred. Men and women left buses east and west of Fifth Avenue. So did cab drivers, their passengers, and other motorists.

Silently and tearfully they stood along the crosswalk. None tried to press forward into Fifth Avenue, although only a few policemen were between them and the approaching hearse. A police sergeant, fighting back his tears, said, "On an occasion like this you don't need discipline."

The quality of the crowd's farewell was caught by a man who stepped aside to allow three little boys to squirm in front of him for a front-row view of the hearse. With a sad smile, he said, "There seems to be gentleness today."

When the procession had passed Forty-second Street, the bus drivers trotted back to the buses to find that none of the passengers had bothered to come back. Some were still standing forlornly, while others were walking slowly to the sidewalks.

Outside Bryant Park, a blind man with an accordion was playing Schubert's "Ave Maria," as the last of the long funeral procession moved south along the avenue.

NORMAN COUSINS
THE SATURDAY REVIEW
June 22, 1968

The ultimate tribute to a man's life is to be found not just in the formal eulogies but in the unspoken and eloquently felt affection of people who own a larger view of the future because of him. In the hours and days just after the murder, numberless testimonials were paid to Robert F. Kennedy by men in high station, in newspaper editorials, and in television and radio commentaries. But none of the attempts to define the meaning of his life said it better than the quiet presence of hundreds of thousands of people who waited in lines in New York City through most of the night and day for a chance to file past a flag-drapped coffin. Long before dawn on Friday, they began to line up near St. Patrick's Cathedral. The line swelled, ten or twelve deep, and backed up two long city blocks to Park Avenue, where it filled the sidewalks and became a solid mass running down the Avenue's east side from Fiftieth Street to Forty-sixth Street, then crossing over to the west side of the street and moving north again for almost a dozen packed blocks.

Robert Kennedy's meaning for these people was hope. He had recaptured hope in situations where it had been broken down so often it had nearly ceased to exist. Park Avenue with its shiny glass and chromium fronts was a universe apart from the black and brown ghettos from which many of the mourners came. There was something symbolic about the contrast, for Robert Kennedy's own wealthy background did not prevent him from going into the ghettos and understanding what they were all about.

The temperature was in the nineties that Friday in New York, and, here and there, building superintendants or tenants on Park Avenue would rig up water hoses and set up a sidewalk oasis. But for most of the people under the sun, there was little or no refreshment. During my half century on this earth, I have seen touching sights beyond forgetting. I have seen a million people stand in massed silent tribute to Mahatma Gandhi. I have listened to Korean refugees singing to each other at night to keep up their spirits. I have seen maimed and disfigured victims of the Hiroshima bombing pray for an end to all war. I have seen compassionate respect and love on the faces of people looking at Jacqueline Kennedy. These are all vivid pictures in the mind and there is now another, of a slow-moving mass of human beings in the heart of Manhattan paying individual respect to a man who had touched them and who had been touched by them.

They were still there on Saturday. The time for filing past the coffin was over; now the great cathedral was ready for the requiem mass. But outside the cathedral, for blocks around, were thousands of people who wanted to come as close as they would be allowed to come to the religious memorial.

The service at St. Patrick's began and Edward Kennedy came forward. One's thoughts turned to the Kennedy brothers, all of them remarkable young men, and now only one left. Ted's accent was typically Kennedyian; so were the words and ideas. You were thankful that Edward Kennedy could still feel as deeply about the future as his brothers had felt, could still talk about the making of a better world, could still ask for rededication, could still have confidence in all the people around him and beyond him. There was much grief to be carried, and he carried it as well as any man could; but he also knew that hopes had to be reborn and that this is what life is all about.

EDITORIAL
THE BOSTON HERALD TRAVELER
June 7, 1968

The death of Robert F. Kennedy cuts all men—young, old, black, white, rich, poor, in this country and others. But it cuts most deeply into his family, a family that has borne unbearable sorrows. To them we offer again our sympathy.

No one could foresee how tragically fate would decide his own future when Robert Kennedy said, "I cannot stand aside from the contest that will decide our nation's future." These words, uttered in the Senate Caucus Room, where his brother before him had stood in a dramatic moment, ended weeks of uncommon and uncomfortable indecision for him.

In the end, Senator Kennedy could not stand aside from a war he saw as destructive to the people of a small country and to the spirit of this large one. He could not stand aside from the widening gulfs of hostility and mistrust between young and old, black and white, left and right. He could not stand aside from his brothers who were hungry.

Thus, as his brother had done before him, Robert F. Kennedy sought a newer world. For a while there were the things that people had seen before—the vigor, the virtue and the victory of a Kennedy campaign. "I think," he said near the finish, "we can end the divisions within the United States." There were smiles, cheers, and hands reaching out. Then suddenly, as had happened to his brother before him, bullets ripped into the dream and killed it.

He will be taken tomorrow past the white buildings of the government he served and, like his brother before him, be laid to rest in Arlington National Cemetery.

Robert Kennedy's impact upon the life of his country was great. It cannot be fully assessed by the normal measurements, though the readily recognizable accomplishments are impressive themselves.

His contributions to the successes of John F. Kennedy's Presidency were considerable. He organized the campaign that put his brother into the White House, helped mold the administration, handled difficult and often unpleasant but necessary political chores, and provided, in the Cuban missile crisis and in other major moments, a voice of cool candor. As Attorney General he speeded prosecution of voting rights and school desegregation cases and helped secure passage of the Civil Rights Act of 1964.

In his own right, Robert Kennedy earned a reputation as a brilliant and aggressive counsel to a number of congressional committees, exposing organized crime's role in labor unions and ordering the investigations that resulted in Teamster President Jimmy Hoffa's conviction on jury-tampering charges.

As U. S. Senator from New York, he urged and supported moves to make private industry's role in solving urban problems larger and the federal government's more effective. In 1967 he introduced two bills to provide tax incentives for investment in poverty areas. Together with community leaders from the Bedford-Stuyvesant area of Brooklyn, the second largest black ghetto in the nation, he organized a community development corporation to successfully test the potential of the private role in poverty.

There are apparent inconsistencies in the career of Robert Kennedy. He was a liberal who served Senator Joseph McCarthy. He was an Attorney General who had never tried a case. He was small, stiff, cool, and not a fluent public speaker, yet his magic drew the largest and most enthusiastic crowds of the 1968 campaign. He was the Democrat who chastised the unions, as well as big business, for disinterest in the social issues that are tearing the country.

It was in part these seeming inconsistencies, perhaps, that drew people to Robert Kennedy. He was not cut from a common die. But his attraction was reinforced by the fact that he was a symbol of something exciting that might be.

There may have been some who followed not a man but a name. There is a fault here, but not a great one because the name Kennedy means something real and special, membership in a cohesive family of continuing dedication, at terrible cost, to public service. The majority, however, followed him not for what he was called but for what he was, not for the image around him but the goals before him. In the recent years and months, it was clear that there were two overriding and complementary concerns—for the war in Vietnam and for the equality and dignity of all men.

In pursuit of this second concern, only he among the candidates could find oneness with what Arthur Schlesinger has called the "constituency of the powerless," the black men and women and children of the ghetto, the dirt poor of Appalachia and the Mississippi Delta, migrant laborers of California and the redmen of the reservations. His demand for justice for these other Americans could not have arisen from expectation of political return, for these people are most often outside the political as well as economic society of America. They loved him because they saw his concern for them was real. The black hands reached out, as they had done before for his brother, across a thousand gulfs to touch a white man who was with them in heart, in mind, and perhaps in "soul." He joined their cause for the same reason he shot the rapids and climbed the mountain. It was there.

Robert Kennedy took the torch of a new generation, and, as his brother before him, sought a newer world. He too died seeking, but as he said, "It is the only way we can live."

EDITORIAL
THE WASHINGTON POST
June 9, 1968

The great thing about the Kennedys is not just that they have courage but that they give it. And the sad thing, which is also the glory of it, is that they give it in greatest measure in the manner in which they meet trial and tragedy.

President John F. Kennedy, his brother Joseph before him, and Senator Robert Kennedy—they all had this grace under pressure. It was everywhere in Senator Edward Kennedy's eulogy to his brother yesterday, full of pride and sorrow, grief and promise. It was in the faces of the children, and the sisters and the mother and the first widow and the second—strained, anguished, composed. It was reflected, in some way, in the faces of the thousands of mourners who had filed past the casket for a day and two nights, touching it as they passed, paying homage, taking strength.

This strength is the special legacy to the nation of the Kennedy who was President and the Kennedy who wanted to be. It does not matter whether they had all the right answers to all the hard questions. What matters is that they had the courage to ask the hard questions about hate and poverty and violence at home and abroad.

The lesson, laid down by Archbishop Terence C. Cooke in his eulogy yesterday, was for us "to find the courage to take up again the laborious work to which Senator Kennedy devoted all his energies." We must find this courage, the Archbishop said, in "the strength that still lies deep within the soul of America." But we will find it also in the legacy, and in the example, of the Kennedys. For it cannot be doubted that those who remain will take up the work of Robert Kennedy, for all their suffering.

That is the Kennedys' chosen way and it does them no honor to see in it, as some have done, the danger of a dynasty. There is no menace in the pursuit of excellence repeated under a common name. There is no peril in profound religious faith, in sound marriages, or good teaching, or fierce family loyalty or a tradition of service by those who by birth could as easily choose a life of ease. If this is dynasty, we would do well to make the most of it, and take the best from it, and the best of it was movingly displayed at the cathedral yesterday, and at the graveside, in the strength and courage of the Kennedy family.

> We must oppose violence not because of what violence does to the possibility of cooperation between whites and blacks; not just because it hampers the passage of civil rights bills, or poverty legislation, or open-occupancy laws.
> The central disease of violence is what it does to all of us—to

those who engage in it as much as to those who are its victims.

Cruelty and wanton violence may temporarily relieve a feeling of frustration, a sense of impotence. But the damage of those who perpetrate it—these are the negation of reason and the antithesis of humanity, and they are the besetting sins of the twentieth century.

Surely the world has seen enough, in the last forty years, of violence and hatred. Surely we have seen enough of the attempt to justify present injustice by past slights, or to punish the unjust by making the world more unjust.

We know now that the color of the executioner's robe matters little. And we know in our hearts, even through times of passion and discontent, that to add to the quantity of violence in this country is to burden our own lives and mortgage our children's souls, and the best possibilities of the American future.

—Senator Robert F. Kennedy in a 1966 speech.

CHARLES FRANKEL
THE SATURDAY REVIEW
June 22, 1968

I knew Robert Kennedy, not intimately but well enough to know the fire of life that was inside him. One felt it immediately. It was tamped down and under control, but it was there as palpably as a bed of coals in a fireplace. He wanted to live with a purpose; he expected that others did too. This was why, whether people liked him or disliked him, it was impossible to feel impersonally about him. And it is one of the reasons his murder hurts so: it seems so impersonal, so purposeless.

What are its implications? At the very least we have lost a man who had qualities that we do not have enough of, either in public life or in our culture at large. Robert Kennedy had a kind of austere passion, a sense of focus and concentration, that is rare and valuable. There was an impatience in him, despite all his awareness of the slow, foolish realities of politics and human nature. He hated to think that there was misery in the world that didn't have to exist. He disliked inefficiency, pomposity, the fraudulent, or the wasteful in talk or thought or action, because he knew the cost of doing things badly. He was disciplined and enduring himself, and he admired disciplined and enduring people. I think this was why he was drawn to athletes, to good writers, to sharp minds, to people who saw what had to be done and did it. He might have made a difference in our national style and the virtues we most admire.

Yet for me these were not his most striking traits. His most remarkable, I thought, were his way of putting his mind forth toward you when you had something important to say and his ability to imagine other people's worlds. He was one of a relatively small number of people whom I have met in public life who really listen. He wanted to hear, and went out of his way to hear, what he hadn't heard before. I think it was this, and not his looks or his youth or his name, that got across to the people in the ghettos and explains their feeling about him. And the deepest political implications of his death, it seems to me, lie not in its effect upon the campaign, but in what it will mean to have this man with his special capacity to listen and to respond removed from the scene.

CHARLES BARTLETT
THE NEW YORK DAILY COLUMN
June 7, 1968

In retrospect it seems only a twinkling of the eye since Robert F. Kennedy, trained and geared for political service but far from fixed on what his role should be, came to Washington at the start of 1953.

He had the strong sense of a young man of high purpose that there was a job to be done but these were Republican days and he was merely the younger brother of a freshman minority Senator. His only option was a staff assignment on the committee then headed by the late Senator Joseph McCarthy and characteristically he set out to make what he could of this slender wedge.

He was not in those days an ideological Democrat. His attention focused on right versus wrong, on honesty versus hypocrisy, on effective action versus vacillation. In his first probe into East-West trade, he was less concerned with whether this trade should go on than with the legerdemain which concealed its scope.

His career was shaped by the abrasive action between his steely sense of the right as he saw it and the politician's inclination to temporize. A first confrontation came in 1955 when he obtained solid evidence of misconduct by the Secretary of the Air Force, Harold Talbott.

The Democratic Senators for whom Kennedy worked were fond of Talbott and embarrassed by the case. They wanted to brush it aside but the young staff man, in a singular display of courage and tenacity, forced the showdown that prompted Talbott's resignation.

His special stamp, a spirit of seeing through a task that needed to be done, carried him into the Teamster Union investigation, which in turn brought him into the heavy waters of controversy.

These long labors in this huge Augean stable gave him his public image with its strengths as well as its weakness, an impression of strong-mindness intense enough to be inexorable.

It is certain that the momentum of the Teamster investigation was an important force in the election of his brother in 1960. It is also certain that he worked slavishly through that campaign without any fixed notion of the role he might play in a Kennedy administration.

Certainly he was far from forward in responding to the idea that he become Attorney General. He balked strenuously in fact until his brother made it clear that he had no choice. He took the job with a slightly glum sense that it was a job to be done, not with any confidence that it would enhance his name.

The next three years were a peak for Kennedy.

The assassination of his brother cruelly halted his opportunity to develop in this ideal setting.

Kennedy's successes in political life were accomplished by his power to muster a headlong commitment, an indomitable force of character. His disappointments derived from his lack of deference to the political graces, his indisposition to float with the crosscurrents of circumstance.

These posed many complexities for him in the period after his brother died. The hostility with Lyndon Johnson was rendered unbridgeable by factors almost beyond the control of either man. The division of the Democrats into camps, the collision of sentiment over the war, and the raucous pace of change posed awesome tests for an emerging politician.

He had great strength, great heart, and a great anxiety to apply the force of his character to the world's advantage. For such a man the sunset should not have come before the afternoon.

WARREN ROGERS
STANLEY TRETICK
LOOK
July 9, 1968

He never understood why some people hated him. After a hard day's campaigning, especially in anti-Kennedy areas, he would sometimes toss the question at us: "Why do they hate me?" Over drinks or a late meal, often long into the night, in his hotel suite or a secluded corner of a nearly deserted restaurant, he liked to ruminate over that or some other question that was troubling him. For him, it was relaxation, the closest he came to idle chatter, a turning away from the public issues he sometimes grew weary of hearing himself talk about. For us, newsmen and staff people, it frequently turned into tough, taxing discussion and debate. He would start an argument, control and direct it, let the rest of us fight it out and, somewhere along the line, jump in himself. But he never could figure out the hate thing. It bothered him, perhaps, because there was no hate in him—not of people. He hated passionately the poverty, ignorance, indifference to human needs, wars, and all of the miseries he inveighed against. But not people. If, as widely implied, there was hate in him early on, he had long since expunged it in the remarkable self-examination and self-improvement regimen he followed over the last several crowded, tortured years, during which he tried to make Robert Francis Kennedy a better man.

One time, we thought we had the answer. Maybe it was his style, his uncompromising demand for vast improvements in our society at great gulps, with no tolerance of stalling. People on the whole, especially when they hold or participate in power, are loath to accept any change. Kennedy's appeal was to the mass of people, the ethnic minorities and the disadvantaged, and that always makes the occupants of the catbird seat uncomfortable. It was slowly dawning on the country that he was something new in American politics: a passionate, compassionate man who genuinely meant what he said. "What you really are is a revolutionary," Stanley Tretick told him once. "You should be in the hills with Castro and Che." There was a pause while he thought about that. "I know it," he said quietly.

No one who really knew him called him Bobby, except for members of his family or boyhood chums grown used to the diminutive. "Bobby's no kid," Senator Jacob K. Javits once observed after watching him pick his way successfully through the brambles of New York politics. It is difficult now to remember when people like us started calling him Bob. It came on gradually. After the brilliant job he did of running his brother's Presidential campaign in 1960, after the gusty performance of the Justice Department while he was Attorney General, after his obvious contributions to coping with the Cuban Missile Crisis and other international problems, it seemed downright silly to continue the child's name. Besides, the years had collected their dues. There were streaks of silver in the bushy mane and lines of worry and suffering in the face.

It seems strange to say it of one born into such wealth, but he was a self-made man. He took a few drinks occasionally and enjoyed a cigar every now and then, yet he never allowed liquor or tobacco to impinge on his superb physical conditioning. He treated his mind and his emotions the same way. He had no time for either ideas or causes that did not promise to enlarge his capacities. Nobody told him to do that or kept tabs on him to see that he did. "As the seventh of nine children in a competitive family, I had to keep getting better in every way just to survive," he once said. Contemplating making a run for the Presidency, and just about decided to do it, he told us: "One of the problems I would have would be meshing the old Kennedy staff with the new. In 1960, my brother did it one way. Now, it's eight years later. What we did then won't work now. It's all different." We talked often about what he called "the hard, hard road ahead." Once, very softly and emphasizing his words with a feigned grimace of pain, he said, "Ooh, what he's going to do to me!" He meant President Johnson, at the time expected to seek re-election. He respected the President's expertise at political infighting. He saw, too, the sheer physical torment that battling through the presidential primaries would bring—the sleepless nights, the decisions under almost intolerable pressure, the racing from one appointment to another. "We're all going to have to work our butts off," he said. "And in the end, it may all be for nothing."

He had the same clear-eyed but stoic insight into the danger of assassination. After he opened his campaign in Kansas in late March, columnist Jimmy Breslin and Warren Rogers were privately chiding him about his lack of security protection and indifference to possible injury in the churning crowds, sometimes turned to mobs, that he attracted. "Oh hell," he said, "you can't worry about that. Look at their faces. Those people don't want to hurt me. They just want to see me and touch me. And if there is somebody out there who wants to get me, well, doing anything in public life today is Russian roulette."

He was a fighter. What a fighter! He would have made a good company commander. Although he spent much of the past two years attacking the Vietnam war and all wars, he had the qualities of a fine military leader. He was a tiger when the fighting began. He took all the chances, assumed all the responsibility, inspired men to take his orders, and always managed to be out in front leading them. "After a few minutes listening to him talk," a veteran in the Army's green-bereted Special Forces told us, "I would follow him anywhere, against any odds, blindly." He had the same effect on his staff members, whose numbers and quality were a source of constant admiration and wonder to his political opponents. Men abandoned their law offices, shut down their businesses, quit jobs they loved so they could devote full time to helping him.

This appeal, in the streets if not in the halls of the mighty, was to all ages, not just to the young. His capacity to empathize, to imagine what it was like to be the other fellow, seemed boundless. A friend once commented, "It's amazing how he understands people. I really believe he knows precisely what it's like to be a little old lady." He certainly knew what it was like to be a little girl: It was Uncle Bobby who protected Caroline during the first trauma-strewn year after her father was assassinated.

The sight of poverty made him physically ill, and he would often rant against the sacrifice of the intelligent poor, the loss of potentially productive citizens, to systematized ignorance. He regretted, perhaps even resented, any human experience denied him. "You're lucky, you were born poor," he once told Warren. He was forever plunging into blighted, economically depressed urban areas like Watts and Harlem for long, secret bull sessions with surly Black Power advocates, and leaving many of the white-hatingest with their bitter convictions shaken.

"You're winning the streets," Stanley told him a few weeks before the fateful California primary. "I've got to win the streets," he said. But, as a political scientist, he was deeply aware of the strong, perhaps decisive, influence of television on politics. While campaigning in the Midwest, at dinner one night he provoked an argument over which was the better technique—his way of personally going to the people, or slick-packaged TV pitches. He argued that his successes were proof that his approach was the most productive. "But you're a political dinosaur, the last we'll probably ever see," Warren said. "And the reason you do it is because you are good at it and you just don't come across on the tube. If you were as good as McCarthy on TV, you'd be arguing for that technique." He rubbed a hand all over his face. "Yeah, I guess you're right," he said. "But we're still going to do it my way."

He collected champions. He liked to be around winners, professionals, whatever the field. That is why he had friends like John Glenn, the first American astronaut to orbit the earth; James Whittaker, the conqueror of Mount Everest, who climbed Mount Kennedy in Canada with him; Rafer Johnson, the track great; and Roosevelt Grier, the legendary tackle of the Los Angeles Rams. Conversely, he could not tolerate phonies or incompetents. He was critical of Senator Eugene McCarthy because, as he said to Stanley after their TV confrontation, "He didn't do his homework." Others were friends because he had shared an experience with them—Whittaker, for example, also qualified because they had suffered together in the snows of Mount Kennedy.

As a news source, he was just about ideal. He almost always found time to talk to people in our business, although he was so on-the-go that talks frequently were in the car, driving back and forth to the airport or between his office and the Senate floor. He trusted newsmen and they trusted him.

He used them as a channel of information and source of criticism that provided an independent check on his own and his staff's analyses and interpretations of events. He managed to maintain friendly personal relations even if, professionally, he and the newsman were at odds. On the day Jacqueline Kennedy sued *Look* magazine, in the celebrated case of her quarrel over publication of excerpts from William Manchester's *The Death of a President*, we were guests at a Christmas party at Bob Kennedy's home in McLean, Virginia. There were no icy stares or calculated snubs. Rather, he seemed to go out of his way to show that while we all were in for a pretty interesting battle, we would be friends again when it was over.

His humor was delightful, not as sophisticated, perhaps, as that of the late President but touched with some of the same whimsicality. He loved being teased by Jimmy Breslin about his speeches. On a day that he had been passionately pleading the cause of the American Indian, quoting statistics on suicide among hopeless youngsters on reservations, Breslin told him, in the privacy of the chartered press plane: "Senator, you killed more Indians today than Warner Brothers. According to you, Jim Thorpe would never have become a sports legend if the rope hadn't broken." We laughed at this nonsensical interpretation for days. Once, signing autographs as the motorcade moved through a California city, he wrote for an astonished young citizen: "Bob Kennedy likes Walt Dumbrow." It was his way of lightening the load of the celebrity trappings he abhorred. Dumbrow, a TV cameraman, rode with him throughout the two and a half months of his presidential campaign, and they became fast friends. He liked to tease Stanley Tretick about the rigors of an election. Early in this campaign, Stanley and a TV cameraman, fighting for position at a speakers platform, were tangled up and just about to come to blows. Kennedy, mounting the stand, saw the whole thing, and Bill Barry, his security aide, called to them. "Take it easy." The fight prevented, the speech over, Kennedy said to Stanley as the motorcade lurched off: "You're slipping, getting soft. In 1960, you wouldn't have hesitated."

He was fun to be around, for many, many reasons. For one, it was never dull. If there was no external excitement, as with a motorcade, he was always ready to discuss or argue. He never pulled rank, although he knew how to put on pressure when he wanted something. He was tough and aggressive—what his foes called "ruthless"—and an unrelenting perfectionist. Yet, as many of us found, he was kind and thoughtful. He was, in short, a giver and not a taker.

Bill Barry, the ex-FBI man who had been holding him on those convertibles for eighty days and who now goes back to his bank vice presidency, told us, his heart aching: "I am a much better man for knowing him than I ever was before." That applies to us, too.

JACK NEWFIELD
THE VILLAGE VOICE
June 13, 1968

It was a little before midnight, a half hour before he was to be assassinated as he reached out to grasp the workingman's hand of a $75-a-week Mexican busboy in the bowels of the Ambassador Hotel.

Robert Kennedy was holding a victory cigar in his swollen and stubby fingers, and squatting on the floor of Room 511. His famous political and intellectual supporters were in the room with him. The awful little pornographers of power were there too. And so were the special people, the victims and rebels Robert Kennedy identified with. Dolores Huerta of the grape strike was there, and Charles Evers, and John Lewis, who once led SNCC, and Budd Schulberg, who runs a writers' workshop in Watts. And Pete Hamill and Jimmy Breslin, two gut journalists who never went to college, but who Kennedy sensed knew more about America than the erudite Lerners, Restons, and Wechslers.

In this last hour, Kennedy seemed the most zestful and most inwardly serene I had seen him since Lyndon Johnson withdrew from the race. When that had happened Kennedy became troubled and confused. He had lost his enemy and his crusade, and he acted like a lost soul, even as he won in Indiana. He seemed, suddenly, to not know who he was.

Defeat in Oregon, and physical exhaustion in California, had gutted his spirit even more. On Sunday he seemed somber and withdrawn as he looked blankly out of the window of his 727 Electra campaign jet. Normally Kennedy would gossip and joke with me on a campaign trip. But on Sunday all he said was that he hoped Al Lowenstein, who was supporting McCarthy, would win his congressional primary fight on Long Island. Then he turned his worn-out face to the breathtaking landscape of California.

On Monday he was drained, and his speeches flat, and he got sick to his stomach in the middle of his final campaign speech in San Diego. The press whispered about a premonition of defeat.

But now, just before midnight, he seemed to be discovering his natural rhythm again, to finally feel liberated from gloom, fatalism, and yes, guilt over not running earlier, and somehow betraying the young he so wanted to lead.

He had won Humphrey's native state of South Dakota and in California. The Indians, and the Mexicans and the Negroes ("my people") had given him his margin of triumph. The turnout of voters in supposedly fragmented, apathetic Watts was higher than in educated, affluent Beverly Hills. Key supporters and aides of Eugene McCarthy had told Richard Goodwin earlier in the night they might now come over to Kennedy's campaign. He had come back from defeat, and won on his own. Robert Kennedy, who was always more Boston than Camelot, once again found the two things he always needed: a cause—the dispossessed—and a clear enemy.

"I am going to chase Hubert Humphrey all over America," he said. "I'm going to chase him into every precinct. Wherever he goes, I'm going to go."

Then he went downstairs carrying his notes for a speech that would attack war and violence.

I spent the death watch in Kennedy's hotel room, watching television, and answering the grieving and bereft phone calls from as far away as London. About twenty people spent the night there, spread out among five or six rooms on the fifth floor. Occasionally a sob or shriek came out of one of the rooms. We drank all the liquor there was, but nobody got drunk.

At about four A.M. Adam Walinsky called from the Hospital of the Good Samaritan to mumble that the outlook was bleak. Then a tape of a speech Kennedy gave at Berkeley attacking poverty and racism flashed on, and I finally broke down. As I wept, two crew-cut employees of the Los Angeles telephone company came into the room, and mechanically began to remove the special telephones that had been installed for the evening, direct lines to the ballroom, and phones used to call South Dakota and Washington. They acted as if nothing was happening, just casually pulling the wires out of the wall, and coiling them around the phones.

In another room in the suite John Lewis, who had campaigned among the hostile, middle class Jews in California, sat on the arm of a chair, tears in his eyes, and mumbling to himself, "Why, why, why?"

John Barlow Martin, his gaunt, Modigliani-like face the color of chalk, said to no one in particular, "Bomb America. Make the Coca-Cola someplace else."

Again and again the television played the drama. Kennedy's last speech, the ballsy challenge to Humphrey, the attack on the war, the jibe at Yorty, and the last awkward victory sign with his two fingers. The moan that broke across the ballroom like a wave. Men and women weeping, praying, pounding the floor. Blair Clark, McCarthy's campaign manager, and columnist Mary McGrory, who loved Bobby almost as much as she loved Gene, came, offered condolences, fought to hold back tears, and left, reeling like sleepwalkers.

At five-thirty A.M. I went downstairs to help pick up Ed Guthman at the hospital. Outside the Ambassador Hotel sat Charles Evers, Medgar's brother. "God, they kill our friends and they kill our leaders," he said. Outside the hospital the press and a few hippies prayed.

Guthman's face said everything. Jimmy Breslin and George Plimpton left the hospital at the same time, and their faces also said that Kennedy's brain was already dead, and only his street fighter's heart kept him technically alive.

Wednesday morning I wandered around the ugly hotel. Scavengers were stealing mementos—campaign hats, banners, posters—from the ballroom.

Now he rests next to his brother, and feelings of rage mingle with a few random personal memories of a soulful man the world thought was ruthless.

Rage at the professional Bobby haters. Not just Joe Resnick or Drew Pearson, but all those reform Democrats and liberal columnists who made hating Bobby so respectable, and even fashionable.

Rage at politicians who now urge passage of the crime bill with its gun-control clause as a "memorial" to Kennedy, even though Kennedy, in life, opposed that legislation because of its provisions for wire tapping and denial of rights to defendants.

Rage at a man like Sam Yorty, who had the Los Angeles police give a traffic ticket to the entire Kennedy motorcade last week, who began red-baiting before Kennedy's heart stopped beating, and who had crashed the funeral, and refused to leave even after being asked to by Jack English.

Rage at men like Archbishop Cooke and Eric Hoffer who say America should feel no national guilt, because the assassin was a Jordanian nationalist. Rage at those eulogizers who never mention the violence of Vietnam, Mississippi, or Texas. Rage at men who cannot face the fact that the truest symbol of America is that lonesome plane from Los Angeles that carried the widows of John Kennedy, Robert Kennedy, and Martin Luther King.

But a few memories linger too. Kennedy quietly reading the Old Testament as a private gesture of irreverence all through the three-hour funeral mass for Cardinal Spellman. Kennedy sitting in his Manhattan apartment and reading me a poem from Emerson. Kennedy visiting a migrant worker camp near Buffalo, and walking right past the manager who held a gun, and into a rotting trailer that was a home for ten migrants. Kennedy pausing while campaigning in Brooklyn in front of a small girl with glasses and suddenly saying, "My little girl wears glasses too. And I love her very much." Kennedy visiting a hospital for retarded children in Westchester last January, and impulsively taking sixteen patients for a ride to buy ice cream, while doctors and aids panicked.

If I had written these things two weeks ago, *The Voice* would have been deluged with letters calling me a whore. Now such anecdotes fill the papers and the networks, and no one doubts them.

When he sent a plane to take Martin Luther King's widow to Memphis, people called it a cheap political gimmick. Two weeks ago I described him being called out of a shower in Indianapolis, and quipping as he groped for the phone, "Make way for the future leader of the Free World." I got a letter saying that proved his arrogance.

Robert Kennedy was not a saint. He was a politician who could talk about law and order in Indiana.

But anyone who rode on his funeral train last Saturday, and looked out at the rows of wounded black faces that lined the poor side of the tracks, knew what might have been. The stone is once again at the bottom of the hill and we are alone.

EDITORIAL
KAYHAN INTERNATIONAL
June 8, 1968

The tragic assassination of Senator Robert F. Kennedy once more spotlights the immense gap between man's achievements in the fields of science and technology and his miserable failure in attaining a morality to match his ever-increasing material strength.

Senator Kennedy fell victim to the kind of violence and inhumanity which he was fighting against. He was determined to eliminate the root causes that breed assassins and set man against man in a brutal bid to negate the very essence of humanity.

Millions of people throughout the world have grieved over Kennedy's senseless murder; they regard his assassination as a blow to the noble causes they cherish, and for which Kennedy was such an eloquent spokesman.

Elimination of injustice and brutality and the quest for equality among all human beings—irrespective of race, creed, and social status—will remain causes for which millions of other men and women will continue to fight, not only in the United States but the world over.

In this age of rapid progress, the urgency of social justice is so strong that real peace will never exist until the ideals for which Kennedy gave his life are fully realized.

We in Iran, who have achieved our tremendous social and political advances only after long and untiring effort know well the value of dedicated leadership. That is why we, too, mourn the loss of a fine man who promised to be a great leader.

INTRODUCTION
EPOCA, SPECIAL EDITION

> And he shall be like a tree planted on the banks of running water, giving fruit in its season, its leaves never fading.   Psalms 1-3

SOLDIER OF THE NEW FRONTIER

This special edition of *Epoca* tells about the most ferocious human violence, but it is also solemn testimony, brought by millions and millions of people around the world, that violence will be overcome and love and harmony will prevail.

They have killed our brother. The name of God always came to his lips and in his heart he cultivated the ideals of freedom and peace. He advocated justice and, because he was a fighter, he never failed to speak out whenever he saw injustice. He was rich and powerful but he never spared himself when it was necessary to make a personal sacrifice. He was young and full of life and yet he did not have the egoism of his young age, which makes people deaf and blind to the fate of the less fortunate. He was loved by his wife, and his ten children, his brothers, his friends and even by those who had been close to him only to shake his hand. He gathered around himself so much love and gave so much of it. The urge to do immediate good made him stronger every day instead of consuming him. He went ahead like a missionary in a land of infidels: he was dreaming of a better world and was trying to build it by example. He also had many enemies who accused him of using the misfortune of others for his own ambition. But the poor, who know true from false, kept saying to him, "You are my brother." Now he is dead. Ignorance and hate were the weapons of his assassin as they were five years ago in Dallas. His name was Robert Francis Kennedy. He lies near John Fitzgerald Kennedy, under the same trees, for the same ideal.

TOM LEATHERS
THE SQUIRE NEWSPAPERS
June 13, 1968

Like most people I know, I wasn't too strong on Bobby Kennedy. I probably never would have voted for him, nor would most of those living out here. The suburbs weren't where he had his strength.

But undoubtedly I would have had a better understanding of him if I had taken the time to read what he was saying while he was alive. But unfortunately we often draw our political conclusions from the obvious, the superficial, the mannerisms, the things that really don't matter. We choose our favorites from something we heard, or something we feel and that's that. Almost nothing the candidate can do can change our mind. He's a good guy or a bad guy and whatever he does in his lifetime won't really make too much difference.

But in death, I got a better perspective of Bobby Kennedy. Now I realize that I may have been a bit hasty in some conclusions. The obvious really wasn't as obvious after all. I remember back to Lawrence, Kansas, a month or so ago when Bobby walked unafraid into a mob of eager, pummeling students. I interpreted his actions as political expedience, since surely no sane person with any other motive would let himself be subjected to such a beating. But the last few days, as I've read some of the Senator's writings and heard what he was saying, I get the feeling that his physical courage reflected a stronger motivation than mere politics. Sure he wanted to get elected, sure he knew how to count the delegates—but I think he had another goal at the end of the rainbow, not just merely being elected to office.

I was particularly impressed by the Senator's statements read at the funeral. Maybe others have a better look at the international problems, at the crisis in Vietnam or maybe a sounder fiscal policy. But for getting to the guts of how you and I can best exist in this very complex life, I'll take the things Bobby Kennedy had to say:

"Some believe there is nothing one man or one woman can do against the enormous array of the world's ills. Yet many of the world's great movements, of thought and action, have followed from the work of a single man. A young monk began the Protestant reformation, a young general extended an empire from Macedonia to the borders of the earth, and a young woman reclaimed the territory of France. It was a young Italian explorer who discovered the New World, and the thirty-two-year-old Thomas Jefferson who proclaimed that all men are created equal.

> "These men moved the world, and so can we all. Few will have the greatness to bend history itself, but each of us can work to change a small portion of events, and in the total of all those acts will be written the history of this generation. It is from numberless diverse acts of courage and belief that human history is shaped. Each time a man stands up for an ideal, or acts to improve the lot of others, or strikes out against injustice, he sends forth a tiny ripple of hope, and crossing each other from a million different centers of energy and daring those ripples build a current that can sweep down the mightiest walls of oppression and resistance."

When those words were read at the funeral, I couldn't help but think of this community right here around us that so sorely needs courageous leadership. Suburban neighborhoods with block after block filled with educated, talented people who have so much more to give than most—but for some reason are holding back and failing to come forth. We tend to pull ourselves inside our houses, pull the shades, and hope that somehow everything will get solved out there around us. But it doesn't.

> "Few are willing to brave the disapproval of their fellows, the censure of their colleagues, the wrath of their society. Moral courage is a rarer commodity than bravery in battle or great intelligence. Yet it is the one essential, vital quality for those who seek to change. And I believe that in this generation those with the courage to enter the moral conflict will find themselves with companions in every corner of the globe."

And then I can't help but see the wide gaps in the meaningful side of our suburban lives. The failure of our governments to face up to the human needs of our community. Johnson County with so many fine things: the schools, the homes, the shopping centers—but with so little of what really counts: the badly needed facilities for mental health, child guidance, family service, alcoholism, youth centers, parks, recreation, etc. Where are the people who will stand up and tell our legislators, our county governments, our cities, that they must face up to what's really going on in our own little world?

> "For the fortunate among us, there is the temptation of financial success so grandly spread before those who enjoy the privilege of education. But that is not the road history has marked out for us. Like it or not, we live in times of danger and uncertainty. But they are also more open to the creative energy of men than any other time in history. All of us will ultimately be judged and as the years pass we will surely judge ourselves, on the effort we have contributed to building a new world society and the extent to which our ideals and goals have shaped that effort."

Just the other day, I received a list of the candidates who have filed for office in the county and state elections this summer. And I got sick at my stomach when I saw candidate after candidate unopposed in Johnson County.

Almost nobody cares enough to challenge anybody. Apparently nobody has a better idea on how to run our governments, nobody has a better approach to getting things accomplished. Or maybe nobody really cares enough to take a chance. Surely we can't really feel that all the men who have served a term or two or even three terms have executed our wishes so perfectly that they can't even be challenged! How can we talk democracy to our children, how can we talk COMMUNITY when we don't have the gumption to become a part of it?

> "The future does not belong to those who are content with today, apathetic toward common problems and their fellow man alike, timid and fearful in the face of new ideas and bold projects. Rather it will belong to those who can blend vision, reason and courage in a personal commitment to the ideals and great enterprises of American society."

Surely in the words of Bobby Kennedy there is a point of motivation for us right here in suburban Kansas City. And for us it should be more meaningful than for those in the ghettos, the underprivileged or the minorities that Bobby Kennedy so often addressed himself to. That's because we have the talent, the time, and the energy to get the things done that Bobby Kennedy is talking about. Call him ruthless, call him cunning, call him politically expedient, Bobby Kennedy, nevertheless, said something to you and me:

> "Our future may live beyond our vision, but is not completely beyond our control. It is the shaping impulse of America that neither fate nor nature nor the irresistible tides of history, but the work of our own hands, matched to reason and principle, that will determine our destiny. There is pride in that, even arrogance, but there is also experience and truth. In any event, it is the only way we can live."

TED LEWIS
THE NEW YORK DAILY NEWS
June 6, 1968

The guy always deserved to be more admired than hated, for he, more than any other Kennedy, was the perfect Irish-American, a gut fighter with brains and a heart that could truly bleed for a cause.

These are the qualities Americans are supposed to most admire in their big-name politicians. Bobby's trouble was that his real self never came through absolutely clear because of the façade of a personality easy to caricature and because of the strange complexities of his inborn character.

He thus, in this year's campaign, either antagonized and disturbed people, or magnetized and aroused them. There never was any middle ground—voters were either firmly for or against. This, incidentally, has historically been true of all great leaders, in political causes or on the battlefields. It is the origin of the old cliché that the enemies a man makes reflects best his stature.

This is the day of all days when it is possible for the nation to be objective about Bobby Kennedy, to think of his attributes rather than his flaws. The tragedy is that it has taken a bullet fired into his brain to make a great many of us take a second look at Kennedy—a clear and sympathetic look, not a jaundiced look.

Consider, for example how he differed markedly from his two brothers, John F. Kennedy and the younger Ted. In any comparison, he lacked the handsome image of either, but had a blood-and-guts quality unequaled by the others. He could hate. He could be, and had been, more ruthless in seeking political advantage. He also was an idealist, a dreamer, a poet at heart, and it is high time that the nation appreciated his sincerity of purpose on the issue of our underprivileged citizens.

He really and truly thought that the country has been going to hell under L.B.J. And agree with him or not on the Vietnam war issue, he believed what he said and had not simply latched on to an issue in order to help him get to the White House.

This is not a maudlin assessment. Neither does it overlook his selfish grasp of the political ladder, his effort this year to push Eugene McCarthy off, and of the carpetbagger indecency that first won him elective office as Senator from New York four years ago.

Even his best friends admit that he was on occasion abrasive, but often just the opposite—jocular, warmhearted, and magnanimous. Larry O'Brien, his key campaign operator, once offered this solid bit about how Bobby ticked:

"The pendulum just swings wider for him than it does for most people."

The truth is that the Irish are exactly that type too. The pendulum swings wider naturally for all those of Celtic origins. They love and hate with great emotion. They are sad and gay with uncontrolled moods. They embrace lost causes on a do-or-die basis.

Perhaps the truest insight into Bobby Kennedy, the man and his mind, has been provided by almost unnoticed off-the-cuff remarks he made to a Negro audience the night of April 4 in Indianapolis.

"I have bad news for you, for all of our fellow citizens...all over the world, and that is that Martin Luther King was shot and killed tonight," he said. "Martin Luther King dedicated his life to love and to justice for his fellow human beings, and he died because of that effort...."

Then Kennedy spoke from his heart, his eloquent spontaneous phrases bringing out into the open the unselfish wellsprings of his political character.

"For those of you who are black and are tempted to be filled with hatred and distrust at the injustice of such an act, against all white people, I can only say that I feel in my own heart the same kind of feeling. I had a member of my family killed, but he was killed by a white man. But we have to make an effort in the United States, we have to make an effort to understand, to go beyond these rather difficult times.

"My favorite poet was Aeschylus. He wrote: 'Even in our sleep, pain which cannot forget falls drop by drop upon the heart until, in our despair, against our will, comes wisdom through the awful grace of God.'

"What we need in the United States is not division; what we need in the United States is not violence or lawlessness, but love, and wisdom, and compassion toward one another, and a feeling of justice toward those who still suffer within our country, whether they be white or whether they be black...."

The final two sentences of that Kennedy speech were most fitting on that April night and they are equally fitting on this day of despair.

"Let us dedicate ourselves," pleaded the young senator, "to what the Greeks wrote so many years ago: to tame the savageness of man and make gentle the life of the world. Let us dedicate ourselves to that, and say a prayer for our country and for our people."

That is what the man said—that ruthless political character, the "opportunist" with a strange hair style.

Which brings us back to what we said far less appropriately after Kennedy was beaten in the Oregon primary a week ago. "The tough little guy" still deserved a hand in our opinion "if for no other reason than that for a few months he put blood and guts into an otherwise dull campaign."

LETTER FROM JUDY ZIMMERMANN
TO MRS. ROBERT F. KENNEDY

June 10, 1968

Dear Mrs. Kennedy:

It was my privilege to have served as an intern in Senator Kennedy's Washington office during the summer of 1965. For all of the young people like myself who shared in the experience of working for and with your husband, he stood as a special example of a man dedicated to public service and to the highest ideals of democracy; justice and equality.

During that summer, as he spoke out for an end to the war; for a halt to the threat of nuclear proliferation; for the needs of the underprivileged, we came to admire him. He often told us that the "good life" was one devoted to the public good, that we should commit ourselves to government service. And so we learned to emulate him. And as, in the course of each day, we alternately bantered or engaged in serious discussion with him, we grew to love him. So it was that we had special cause for delight when last March Senator Kennedy announced he would enter the presidential race. Immediately, we enlisted in the cause of that great last campaign.

An unspeakable tragedy has dealt us all a stunning blow in the senseless, grievous crime which took the life of Robert Kennedy. His loss is irreplaceable and we mourn deeply with you. No other leader offers the ideals and compassion, the commitment and the promise of Robert Kennedy.

But I pray that it may be of some small comfort to you and your dear family to know that, though he gave his life, he did not die in vain. For his principles and dedication shall be guidelines to the rest of us for as long as we live. In the words of the poet Aeschylus:

> May the Gods grant
> Divine favor to our champion,
> Since justly he comes forward
> A fighter for us.

Sincerely,

Judy Zimmermann

LETTER FROM MRS. GERTRUDE CLAFLIN
TO MRS. ROBERT F. KENNEDY

June 6, 1968

Dear Mrs. Kennedy:

Perhaps you may never get to read this letter, but I pray that you will. I am an Indian mother with a son in the Navy and two small children at home. I am one of the poor Indians that your wonderful husband cared about. I live on the Allegany Indian Reservation, a part of the Seneca Nation that you visited last year. At that time he was made a member of our tribe and a member of the Wolf Clan, my clan, too.

As one of the people that your husband cared about, may I tell you what he meant to us?

He was "white"...he was "rich"...by "white" I mean that he was DECENT. By "rich" I mean that was WISE. He knew of our shoddy treatment and he knew of it first hand, for he went to our people and saw what we had or didn't have. And HE CARED. He tried to do something about it.

He gave us hope last year. Hope that our Seneca Nation would not be terminated came from him. At that point, we didn't know where to turn. From that time last year, we began to live again. He saw how much our land and identity meant to us. So few did.

With him as our Senator, we felt secure...just knowing that he would be there to help us...he would be there when and if the Termination Bill would come up.

Then he announced that he was running for the President. We were overjoyed. Many of us staunch Republicans committed our votes to Our Protector. Some who had never voted before were going to...to vote for Bobby. We all saw hope that the war would come to an end and we would have our minds eased, knowing our sons would not be facing guns. We felt hope for "our country"...the U.S. We felt hope...for our proud identity and that we could keep our dignity. Each day of his campaign, we all loved him more.

What we feel now is despair. We feel hatred for HATE. We feel sorrow for the people who couldn't see this wonderful man as an Indian saw him... good, kind, loving, compassionate.

We feel envy, for you. You knew him as no other did. You loved him as no other did. We also feel sorrow for you. Sorrow that you had to lose him to such an ugly act...something he deplored.

We loved him, too, Mrs. Kennedy. Loving a public official for an Indian is almost unheard of, as history bears out. We trusted him. Unheard of, too, for an Indian. We had faith in him.

I hope that you have read this personally, but if you haven't, at least I have put on paper the feelings we had for this man. The hurt I have had has eased by getting this down.

    We know a little of what you feel; we feel it, too. One of our richest experiences was having you both on our reservation, caring about us. Yours was being Mrs. Kennedy. May God be with you and give you all the strength you need.

Sorrowfully,
Mrs. Gertrude Claflin

June 12 1968

Dear Mrs. Kennedy
   We must stop the shooting our best men.
Now he is in heaven.
So all the people crowded his grave.
We Loved him so much then someone
Killed him, so we buried him.
We are so sorry.
Love, Anthony C. Germano age 7

Be cause I want you be happy,
I am sending this penny.

AFTER 5 DAYS RETURN TO
Anthony Germano
22 Williams St.
Salem, mass
01970

LYNN, MA
JUN 10
5 PM
1968

PRAY
FOR
PEACE

Mrs. R. Kennedy
Hyannis Port, Mass.

LETTER FROM JOHN W. DOUGLAS
TO MRS. ROBERT F. KENNEDY

July 4, 1968

Dear Ethel:

After some hesitation I decided to go ahead and write this letter. Perhaps, when the younger children grow up they might like to look at it.

I could not have asked for a finer friend than Bob. If he had never held a public position or shouldered heavy official responsibilities, he would still have been, for me, a magnificent human being and a wonderful friend. This is the man about whom I write.

He was, first of all, a model of rectitude in his personal relationships—in this respect, one of the most fastidious men I've ever encountered. In all his dealings he was straightforward, candid, and direct. He was absolutely reliable. He never dissembled, never trimmed on his word, undercut a colleague or a subordinate.

He was a strong competitor, but he never cut a corner or took an unfair advantage. He never did anything in private which he was unwilling to defend in public. He never asked others to do things which he was unwilling to do himself.

He was thoughtful and considerate toward those with whom he worked. He remembered his friends regardless of their position or status. He was intensely human—concerned with the other person's interests, sympathetic and compassionate, discreet and understanding. He was a generous person. When he thanked you for something, you had no doubt that he really meant it.

Bob neither ducked responsibility nor tried to shift blame. He stood up for his subordinates, deliberately sought to give them some of the limelight, and repaid loyalty with a loyalty more intense than that he received. And by according to those with whom he worked that sense of mingled respect, understanding, and trust, he generated in them a feeling of enhanced confidence and a sense of participation in things important which enabled them to perform above that level of competence and dedication which even they had felt was the limit of their reach.

With all of his strong virtues one would have understood and forgotten, as irrelevant, if Bob had been either standoffish or superior. But there wasn't a trace of either in his make-up. He was a delightful companion, modest, engaging, alert, and great fun. And while his own standards of conduct were impeccable he was, contrary to the popular notion, tolerant of others' shortcomings, anxious to see and encourage the best in them.

There was, for me, no difference between the private man I knew and the public man I observed. Here was a resolute, cheerful leader with high ideals and a firm sense of purpose and conviction, a man of courage and compassion, of determination and dedication, energetic and intelligent, broad-minded and far-sighted, principled and tolerant, vibrant and growing, with a passion both to excel and to improve the lot of others, particularly the less fortunate. There was nothing mean or petty in his make-up or outlook. Thoughtful, understanding, brilliant, witty, and reflective, he never flinched, but instead pressed on for his beliefs and convictions.

Bob was, indeed, a magnificent friend, a wonderful man to work for and to work with. And if, as I think is the case, a valid test of a nation's worth lies in those personal qualities which it tends to foster in its own citizens, then there can be no finer goal for our society than to encourage those qualities of character and mind which Bob had in such abundance. Those who knew Bob and those who worked with him are far better men for that association. Certainly, I count myself doubly honored by reason of having been in that fortunate company.

Love,

John

© 1968 FRANCE-S

LETTER FROM INMATES OF SAN QUENTIN
TO MRS. ROBERT F. KENNEDY

June 28, 1968

Mrs. Robert Kennedy,
c/o The United States Senate Building
Washington 25, D.C.

Dear Mrs. Kennedy:

We, the men here in San Quentin, both State and Federal prisoners alike, are writing you this letter to show our deepest heartfelt sorrow for the loss of your husband, and the loss of a great American.

We here, who are now, or have been, Federal prisoners, or those of us who have at one time or another had dealings with The United States Attorney Generals Office know of the deeds and accomplishments of your husband, to help to insure those that have been or are accused of a crime, in either State or Federal courtrooms, of fair and equal treatment. He was a man who fought hard, but he fought fair, and it was by his actions and through his efforts that we have been assured of a fair and honest hearing and trial. He, to us, did things that we did not really understand or agree with, but we feel that he fought for the things that he felt were best for his country.

Some of us here were among the first who have benifited in some way by the work program that he initiated. It was his feelings and ideas that to put a man to work, even tho incarcerated, he, the prisoner, could and would feel, that even tho down, he was still of some use to himself, his family, and to society, he gave back to the prisoners some of the self respect that is lost by incarceration.

It was with shocked silence that this institution, as well as others, received the news, first of the shooting, and then of the passing of Mr. Kennedy. We have in the past decade, been witness to many things, and among these were the three great tragedies of our time, first the Assassination of your Brother-in-law and our late President, John F. Kennedy, then the Assassination of one of the great Negro leaders of our time, the late Rev. Dr. Martin Luther King Jr., and now the Assassination of your husband, and one of the great friends of the under-privileged, the poor, the accused, and the convicted, Mr. Robert Kennedy. These acts, to me, as well as to many of our nation, were senseless and irresponsible acts committed by persons who did not and would not bother to use the common sense that they were born with.

We here, along with the society outside, can only hope and pray that the persons who preach hatred and bigotry, will soon stop and realize, that all men are created equal, and that we must all learn to live together on this earth, as human beings, and that the past tragadies of our times must not reoccur, if this great nation is to survive.

We therefore close hoping that you will accept our deepest and humblest sympathy, and know that our hopes and prayers for peace and freedom are with you now in this time of trouble, and that we feel a great sorrow and at a great loss at the passing of a man.

We remain respectfully

Yours,

The Inmates and Men of San Quentin

RICHARD HARWOOD
THE WASHINGTON POST
June 7, 1968

A few days after Robert Kennedy became a presidential candidate, the people traveling with him noticed that late at night, slouched in an airplane seat, his hands would sometimes tremble.

It took a while to figure out that it was not fatigue but the emotions that churned around inside him in those early days. He had then a very simple and a very plebian problem. It was stage fright. He wasn't sure of himself as a performer.

His voice was often too shrill. His words were often ill-chosen. He talked too long and got argumentative in question-and-answer sessions with his audiences.

The reason, one of his oldest social friends said, was that Robert Kennedy "lives too closely to the surface. He is a very emotional man, the most compassionate of all the Kennedys. He's got more heart than mind."

In the ten weeks that followed and took him through the primaries in Indiana, Nebraska, Oregon, and California the tremor in the hands disappeared, the shrillness left his voice, and he became the happiest of warriors. He kidded himself constantly for being "ruthless" when the common judgment was that he was far too soft-hearted for his own good.

That may have been an oversimplification. One of his staff members said before Indiana that there really was a "good Bobby and a bad Bobby," and that the "bad Bobby" was like the petulant baseball player who strikes out in the clutch and then kicks the bat boy.

But that side of him rarely surfaced. What came out most in the bull sessions with reporters late at night, in his public appearances, and in his private behavior, was his gentleness.

His capacity for affection was striking. Children appealed to him most. He admired athletes and heroes and seemed most comfortable with people like John Glenn, the astronaut, and Roosevelt Grier, the professional football player.

There was a special affection for his cocker spaniel, Freckles, who traveled everywhere with him and often slept by his side.

What moved him most, though, was life in the ghetto, in eastern Kentucky, in the Delta of Mississippi and on the Indian reservations.

The poor outsiders of this world became an obsession with him. He saw himself as their only authentic champion. And from the hysterical way they greeted him and from the enormous vote majorities they gave him, it was fairly obvious that the blacks and the Indians and the Mexican-Americans saw him that way, too.

Talking about them in an Indiana speech one day, he got so choked up he had to sit down. Many people in the audience were crying because of his passion and eloquence.

He wasted none of it on himself. There were no tears and no self-pity after his defeat in Oregon by Eugene McCarthy. Instead, he joked about Freckles costing him the election. In every discussion of his political future he was fatalistic and not at all cocksure. His estimation of himself was that "maybe we can do something." That was about all he ever said on that subject.

One thing that impressed itself on his crowds, wherever he went, was his size. People were always saying how "tiny" he was, but that was a relative thing. Although only five feet nine and weighing only about 150 or 160 pounds, he had powerful shoulders and forearms and was a very physical man —mountain climbing, football, swimming. His stamina in this campaign was enormous; eighteen to twenty hour days were common. But he kept himself in good shape—no heavy drinking, only an occasional cigar, and a capacity for instant sleep.

If he had any premonitions of disaster, he never showed it. In Salt Lake City early in the campaign, the police warned him of a bomb threat in an auditorium in which he was to speak. He showed up and joked about the anxiety. He joked about an abortive take-off in a chartered airplane one day and in a little town in West Virginia a few weeks ago, showed not a flicker of emotion when a rifle shot rang out from the nearby hills.

His wife was less sanguine. In San Francisco's Chinatown on Monday, the Kennedys were riding in an open car when a string of firecrackers was set off. The Senator called to a reporter running behind his car and asked him to get aboard. What he wanted was someone to hold Ethel's hand. She had been frightened.

An hour or so later he was racing down a freeway to the airport. His old friend, John Seigenthaler, editor of the Nashville *Tennessean*, was in the car. They began singing a song in Japanese at the top of their voices. Ethel joined in. They sang and sang and no one would ever have known that he was twenty-four hours away from a primary election that could make or break him or that he was only thirty hours away from a rendezvous with a man with a gun.

RICHARD HARWOOD
THE WASHINGTON POST
June 8, 1968

The old illusions about Robert Francis Kennedy have probably died with him—the illusions of ruthlessness, coldness, and cant.

And new illusions, as in the case of his dead brother John, may soon take their place—larger-than-life illusions of grandeur and gallantry.

No one is served by that.

In some ways, he was a simple man. One of his friends said not long ago that he ought to be remembered as a partner in one of the great love affairs of our time. His relationship with his wife was, in a word, beautiful. They were in love with each other, with their children, and with the life they shared.

He found it almost impossible to make a speech without some affectionate reference to all that. He found it impossible to campaign for any long period of time without someone there from home. So his wife went with him much of the way although she lived in constant terror of airplanes.

Kennedy was simple in other ways. David Abbott a correspondent for the Canadian Broadcasting Co., once said that Kennedy had both the hands and the taste of an Irish peasant. He liked physical things—football, swimming, and running—and liked people who could do them well.

Like a lot of other people, Fred Dutton, his friend and campaign manager, had private reservations about Robert Kennedy at the beginning of his campaign for the Presidency. But as the weeks passed, those reservations disappeared and just before the Senator was killed he said to a friend: "I'm certain now that he is the kind of guy I'd like in a foxhole with me. He wouldn't run when the shooting started." Everyone around him got to feel that way.

His intellectual gifts were not spectacular. He was no original philosopher. As an orator and as a thinker he often left something to be desired.

But he talked·the language and felt the feelings of ordinary people and had, beyond that, the gift for laughter. He was always laughing—with his crowds, with his friends, with newsmen. He couldn't resist the impish joke or the self-mockery that his extravagant critics inspired. They talked in outraged language about his money, his ambition, his ruthlessness. To him, it was all something to laugh about and to kid himself about and he did it constantly.

Kennedy had another quality that may have had something to do with what has been called his "charisma." He loved and respected children of all ages, and young men too.

So he wore his hair long—at least until the Indiana primary—and surrounded himself with articulate, fuzzy-faced boys who spoke or seemed to speak for the generation that was coming along. Adam Walinsky, at thirty-one, had far more influence on the course of his thought and the development of his political theories than such elder intellectuals Theodore Sorensen and Arthur Schlesinger Jr.

The night of the Indiana primary he finally ate dinner at two A.M. at an airport restaurant and ran into some of the college students who had been working for Eugene McCarthy. He took them along to eat, talked to them for hours, and the next day said: "Gosh, those kids are great. They're just marvelous."

Besides the family and the kids, he had a special relationship and a special affection for newspaper reporters and other people who are the rank and file of the mass media in this country. Jimmy Breslin, one of his pals, wrote: "If you had to work for a living and you wound up around Robert Kennedy to do this work, you wound up with one of your own. And everybody knew he was going to be shot somewhere along the line...."

He was right on the first point. Robert Kennedy seemed like one of your own which means that he was not pompous, that he took himself less seriously than his enemies took him, that he talked easily and without extravagance late at night, and that he was full of whatever human quality it is that makes one man say to another, "You're all right."

Dick Tuck, the elfish advance man in the Kennedy organization, took the press badges one day and pasted on them a Spanish phrase from the cards people put down when they want to reserve a seat on an airplane. The phrase was "Viajando juntos" which means, approximately, "traveling together."

A lot of other people felt that way about Robert Kennedy.

ROBERT HEALY
THE BOSTON GLOBE
June 6, 1968

In the lobby of the Ambassador Hotel, the tall blond woman and her escort heard the news that Robert Kennedy has been shot. They smiled at each other.

Early Thursday morning, coming back from the Good Samaritan Hospital after it had been announced that Senator Kennedy had died, a reporter told a colleague that he felt sorry for the ten Kennedy children; that they would miss him most.

A black cab driver heard it and turned around: "I'm sorry mister, but a lot of kids in the street are going to miss him even more."

It was like that with Robert Kennedy.

They either loved him or they hated him. There was no in-between.

Part of this stems from the fact that he understood deeply those who had been left out when the good things of the world were passed around and he spoke up for them.

Charles Evers, Mississippi Negro leader and the brother of the slain Medgar Evers, was with him the night he was shot. He said Kennedy was the only white man that he could trust. "He was like my brother."

But Evers knew him. The testimony of those who did not know him as well was even more striking. On Monday night Kennedy rode through the Watts section of Los Angeles. He was like the Pied Piper. Small children pedaled their bikes as fast as they could to keep up with him. A big, fat old lady jumped up and down screaming: "Bless him . . . bless him . . . bless him."

And when they reached out to touch his hand they felt they had touched the President of the United States. At least he was their President.

A lot of white people in the country are going to realize someday that they are going to need a white man that the Negro can trust.

But his appeal was not limited just to the blacks. He proved in at least three primaries this year that he appealed to the lower-income white group... again some of those who have been left out of the good things of the world.

A good many political writers would have said this is because he was an Irish Catholic. And indeed the suppression and prejudice his forebears met might have played their part. But the poor also believed that he could help them; that he would listen to them.

Robert Kennedy was the moralist in the Kennedy family. His brother John made accommodations to politics much more easily than he did.

His only major accommodations to politics was when he refused to run against Lyndon Johnson. And it bothered him. Because there was no one with a deeper conviction against the Vietnam war and what it was doing to the nation.

Robert Kennedy was always first down the rapids and first up the mountain. He did not like the idea of being second in this moral challenge. From the period of December when Eugene McCarthy got into the race until he himself entered in March, this gnawed at him.

And even after he got in, he said in a private conversation: "This may not be my time." But he was doing what he wanted to be doing. He was talking about the people in the cities and about their problems. And when some of his advisers told him that the problems of the cities were remote to the voters of Oregon and might cost him votes in the primary if he continued, he did not change.

He loved his brother John—a good trait in a man. He was so unsparing in this that he took with relish some of the blows that might have been aimed at his brother. John Kennedy was much tougher than Robert Kennedy. But it was always Robert that they called ruthless.

Sometimes people had great difficulty talking to him. He would go silent. And yet, there was never a time that Kennedy had trouble talking to a ten or a twelve year old.

Robert Kennedy then was someone to whip and someone to love. He was a good man.

ANTONIO ORENDAIN
EL MALCRIADO*
June 15, 1968

> "I walked a mile with pleasure,
> She chattered all the way,
> And left me none the wiser,
> For all she had to say.
>
> "I walked a mile with Sorrow,
> And not a word said she.
> But oh, the things I learned from her,
> When Sorrow walked with me."
>
> —Robert Browning Hamilton

We ought carefully to consider these words, for they give us the strength and courage we need to continue in our struggle.

We farm workers have labored with a new determination in recent months, because there was a beacon which guided us much as the lighthouse guides the sailor on a stormy night. That beacon was Kennedy—a beacon of hope for the farm worker. Who, except him, had come to the bottom of the pit to bring hope and encouragement to the farm worker? It was he who gave us new spirit.

It was he who said there was a place in the social order for farm workers, and that there would be new laws to help us gain entry into this great society and so-called democracy. It was he who told us he would work for these laws, and that promise was more than anyone else had ever given us.

Above, I used the phrase, "The bottom of the pit" because he came to us when we needed him most, long before he began his tragic adventure. May our friend Rest in Peace. His walk with us was like a fleeting star or a flash of lightning in a black and gloomy night. But that short-lived light gave us direction. We identified with him as workers in the same Cause.

Today there is again darkness, but we know we are further along on the road to justice. We are stronger because we have united to regain the heritage the growers have robbed from us.

We have decided to regain our rights, and so we shall, for, "It is better to die on your feet than to live on your knees." Perhaps some of us will follow the path that Kennedy was made to follow, but we are ready for that journey if it is necessary. The destiny of the farm worker must now change. We will have justice.

"AN HONORABLE PROFESSION"

Senator Robert F. Kennedy did not die in vain, for either they will give us our rights or begin to select their victims from among us. The life of the farm workers today is like "imagining a group of chained men, all condemned to death, some of whom are beheaded daily in the presence of the others, who wait, hope lost, their own turn." Such is the life of the campesino.

*Publication of the Farm Workers

SIMEON BOOKER
JET MAGAZINE
June 20, 1968

It happened several weeks after the assassination of President John F. Kennedy. I got a call to come over to the Attorney General's office. Entering the office of the Justice Department head, I underwent a moving experience. At his huge desk, the Attorney General covered his head in his hands and when he lifted his head, I reasoned he had been crying. His eyes were red and wet. "Come on now," I told Attorney General Robert Kennedy. "You've got to forget the past, I said, "Hell, you're Irish and supposed to be tough. I'm Negro and you think you can push me around." The words jolted the Attorney General and he smiled saying, "Booker, you always know how to knock somebody off balance."

In almost twenty years of covering the nation's capital I have known no public figure as warm and friendly as New York Senator Robert Kennedy. As a reporter in competition with a combined white press of newspaper, radio, and television, I found few of the VIPs even considerate of the black press, few willing to accept me as a working newspaperman and invite me to confidential briefings and to dinners at their homes. Robert Kennedy was the exception. He was the first Cabinet member to invite me to briefings, to his home for a swim, and on airplane trips that he thought would make good articles for *Jet* and *Ebony*. The passing of a friend is the usual time for an avalanche of words in testimony to his determination and courage. But this is not the place for the melody of words. Bob Kennedy would better appreciate friendship—in stride without editorializing.

During the 1960 political campaign, I first met Bob Kennedy. He was the strategist for the vote thrust of his brother and I was the only Negro reporter on the campaign trail. After serving almost two months on the road, I arrived in Hyannis Port, Massachusetts, for the election night count only to find that my hotel was almost five miles from the armory. Raising hell about the disregard of seniority, I finally got better quarters, thanks to Bob Kennedy and Andrew Hatcher, the press secretary. Later, Bob Kennedy told me he "understood the point" of my beef and on Inauguration Day, I was the first Negro ever to be selected as one of eight reporters to ride down Pennsylvania Avenue behind an incoming President.

But as a reporter, I refused to succumb to the Kennedy charm. Early, I turned down White House invitations and began the job of crusading for more opportunities and advantages for Negroes, always using my friendship with Bobby as a course for action. During the Freedom Ride following the bus burning in Anniston, Alabama, I raced to the home of Reverend Fred Shuttlesworth to alert them to send cars to pick up stranded members of our interracial team being beaten in the bus terminal. At the height of the turmoil, a secretary handed me the phone and said, "The Attorney General is on the phone." "What are you doing down there?" started off the younger Kennedy. "It's hell," I retorted. "These people need help." A few hours later, the Justice Department dispatched a plane to pick up the stranded Freedom Riders.

After a dinner late at his Hickory Hill home in Virginia, Bobby stood on the porch to bid good-bye. "You'd better duck inside," I jibed, "before real estate values decrease." The Attorney General shook his head in confusion. During the trip to the Ivory Coast for an independence celebration, the Attorney General got stranded in a throng of Africans. "Just hold on to me," I joked him. "You can never find your way among blacks." But Senator Robert Kennedy found his way among blacks and whites, and he created a course that was the promise for millions. He respected no establishment, black or white, because he knew that in the long run the little people would decide any issue. Perhaps, that is why there is little need for a long memorial piece. What Bobby did and accomplished is written into the hearts and minds of the thousands of people he came into contact with—including this black reporter.

THOMAS B. CONGDON, JR.
THE SATURDAY EVENING POST
June 29, 1968

This is not an intimate memoir. I did not know Robert Kennedy for a long time, or very personally. But perhaps nevertheless I knew him well. I don't know. That is the point of this piece: the awful problem for outsiders of knowing who Robert Kennedy was. The question was obsessively important to Americans this election-year springtime, and will be for many years to come. "I talked with some of the people in the Kennedy crowds," a reporter said to me in Indianapolis. "They barely mention McCarthy, they barely mention Governor Branigan. It all boils down to whether you like Bobby Kennedy or whether you hate Bobby Kennedy."

At first I did neither. I had merely a distrust for the true believers who clustered around him. For me the Kennedy mystique seemed vaguely sinister, a mixture of guile and propaganda. But almost suddenly, in 1965, Robert Kennedy began to make remarkable speeches from the floor of the Senate, addressing himself with passion and candor to the nation's bitterest problems —the powerlessness of the poor, the agony of slums, the inadequacy of stubborn anti-Communism as the ultimate principle of foreign policy. No other major political figure was talking this way.

So I wrote him a letter and said that as national-affairs editor of this magazine I would have some part in determining how to cover him, and I wanted to do it accurately, not in response to clichés. A lunch was arranged at Christ Cella, a well-bred steak house in Manhattan's East 40s, and I was warned that the Senator could spare only forty-five minutes. I was early and he was late, but eventually he dashed in, and we went to the upstairs dining room and had chef's salad and bottled beer. We talked about his wife's sister Ann, a pretty blonde I'd known as we grew up in the same Connecticut town. We talked about his assault on Mount Kennedy, in Canada. "A reporter from *Time* visited us at base camp," he said, "and brought us some steaks and a bottle of Madeira—and then filed a story accusing us of too much luxury for mountain climbing.... He said we feasted on steaks and Madeira!"

The conversation turned serious, and he began to cover the issues he had been speaking upon in the Senate. And as the lunch slid past the forty-five-minute mark, past an hour and then past two hours, I not only listened to Kennedy but watched myself, wondering if I too was being beguiled. For in two and a half hours of strenuous give-and-take I did not detect one fraudulent note, one trace of faked concern, one demagogic trick.

Actually, it didn't enormously matter whether or not I was beguiled, because the articles in the *Post* are by-lined, and the opinions are the authors', and usually the most an editor will do is raise persuasive questions. A few of our subsequent Kennedy articles were somewhat admiring, others were somewhat critical.

Early in the morning of April 22, I boarded the Kennedy campaign plane in Washington, bound for the Indiana primary campaign. The fifty or sixty reporters and photographers sat in the plane and waited, and then the Senator and his wife and three of their children came aboard—blue eyes and freckles. The Senator sat across the aisle from me and smiled and said, "We're using only the best briefing material," pulling out a 1953 copy of *The Saturday Evening Post* with an article on Indiana by John Bartlow Martin. Later, Ethel scanned the article and then passed it to their daughter, Courtney, saying, "Here, learn something about where you're going."

Where we were going was southern Indiana, "Nixon country." The weather was beautiful—"It's a nice day in America," said one reporter from New York, stepping onto the heartland soil—but the day went sour almost immediately. Kennedy was taken to the Ramada Inn, a motel in Vincennes, where perhaps 100 members of the local men's service clubs were assembled. Kennedy was late, and the club members had started their meal, and they continued it as he spoke, their eyes on the Salisbury steak instead of the candidate. He gave a version of his standard speech, but he was strained and formal. There were questions about his views on gun control and the *Pueblo* incident and "God's time"—federally imposed Daylight Saving Time had infuriated Indiana farmers. Kennedy, unfortunately, had no opinion on God's time; it was obvious he had never given it a thought.

Then, turning a vague question to his own purpose, he gave up all notion of speaking to the audience on the matters that concerned it most—such as law and order—and instead tried to stir it with the matters that most concerned him. To the club members—big, heavy men, most of them, well-fleshed and still occupied in shoveling in their lunch—the Senator from New York spoke of children starving, of "*American* children, starving in *America*." It was reverse demagoguery—he was telling them precisely the opposite of what they wanted to hear.

"Do you know," he asked, voice rising, "there are more rats than people in New York City?"

Now this struck the club members as an apt metaphor for what they had always believed about New York City, and a number of them guffawed.

Kennedy went grim, and with terrible deliberateness said, "*Don't . . . laugh. . . .*" The room hushed. There were a few more questions, and finally he escaped to confused applause.

But the days that followed were progressively better. The crowds grew and were enthusiastic. BOBBY HAS SOUL, said a sign. BOBBY YOUR [sic] GREAT, said another. Said a third: SO WHAT IF HIS HAIR IS A SILLY MILLIMETER LONGER!

The enthusiasm made Kennedy blossom. "I am very happy to be in

Wabash," he said after being introduced by the mayor of that town, "and I want to say how grateful I am for the courtesy of your mayor—standing there with his Nixon button."

In Huntington someone presented him with a pot of petunias. "I am very happy to be in Petunia," he said. "I have always wanted to come to Petunia." The crowd loved it. It was a nice moment.

We were all beguiled, and we knew it. There was plenty of press wisecrackery about Kennedy, however—for example, the jokes about his maddening habit of ending every speech with the words, "As George Bernard Shaw once said . . ." followed by a Shaw quote that never failed to bewilder his audience. Or about the ubiquitous high school band playing *This Land Is Your Land* as the motorcade rolled up to the courthouse steps. ("This land is *my* land," a radio announcer said in a perfect imitation of Bobby the Ruthless. "If you don't elect me President, I'm going to pick up my country and take it away.")

One day's schedule called for Kennedy to retrace the route of the famous old Wabash Cannonball, the train celebrated in the ballad of the same name. His staff had hired a train with a rear observation platform, and stops were to be made in the little towns along the tracks. In the press car, some of the best journalistic talents of the nation occupied themselves between stops by composing a parody of the Wabash ballad, entitled "The Ruthless Cannonball." Finally, the Senator was summoned to hear the finished version; Frank Mankiewicz, the Senator's Press Secretary, brought him back to the press car, not really wanting to, but not wanting to have Kennedy appear a bad sport either. A young reporter with a good voice had brought along his guitar and struck a cord.

I was sitting in a camp chair in the aisle, and Kennedy came up behind me and stopped, and put his hands on my shoulders. The song began. I couldn't see his face, but I could feel his fingers pressing me as he listened, the pressure never relaxing.

> Oh, listen to the speeches
>   that baffle, beef, and bore
> As he waffles through the woodlands
>   and slides along the shore.
> He's the politician
>   who's touched by one and all.
> He's the demon driver
>   of the Ruthless Cannonball.

It doesn't look mean, reading it now as I copy it from my notebook, but at the time it seemed too biting. (Was it the assassination aura?) The song went on for seven stanzas, which seemed too many, and concluded with:

> So here's to Ruthless Robert
> May his name forever stand
> To be feared and genuflected at
> by pols across the land.
> Ho Chi Minh is cheering,
> And though it may appall,
> He's whizzing to the White House
> on the Ruthless Cannonball.

It ended, and there was silence as everyone turned to Kennedy for his reaction. His hands still on my shoulders, his voice coming from just above me, he said at last, "As George Bernard Shaw once said...".

Wild laughter, partly in relief that he had taken it lightly.

"As George Bernard Shaw once said," he repeated, "the same to you, buddy."

More laughter, and applause. And suddenly the hands were gone, and so was he.

I seemed to be a little amazed that I can no longer feel the fingers on my shoulders. I remember feeling the feeling, but the feeling itself is gone, and somehow, half consciously, I had half expected it would not go. What is much more vivid is a series of small impressions not of Kennedy at all but of people responding to Kennedy. The telephone lineman on a pole across a field, swinging his yellow hard hat in a jubilant arc as the candidate's convertible passed by. Brightly dressed children streaming from a brick elementary school out in the flat farmland, running across a dandelion-speckled lawn toward the man they all knew.

And the burly south Indiana farmer who caught Kennedy coming out of a crossroads store and stopped him with a blunt question. I couldn't hear the question or the reply. But as Kennedy talked I saw the man change. He was twice the girth of Kennedy, with the big belly of the prosperous workingman; next to him, Kennedy's frame looked meager, his stomach almost concave. Clothes, hair, gestures—they seemed a world apart, and I wondered how these men of girth, to whom manhood connotes a certain fleshy amplitude, could relate to this wispy Easterner, let alone vote for him. The fact is, though, that Kennedy carried southern Indiana. I saw it happening, for during that unheard conversation, the farmer slowly relaxed and then smiled, and then—as Kennedy broke off the conversation by patting the farmer briskly on that belly—he beamed, revealing two fine gold front teeth.

Seven weeks later I again saw Kennedy among the people, the thousands upon thousands of mourners who streamed past his bier in St. Patrick's Cathedral. It was three A.M., and a new honor guard was due to relieve the previous guard, but one member was absent; and so a Kennedy staff man I knew nodded to me, and I went and stood at the foot of the coffin. My hands were clasped in front of me, and because the space was cramped, my fingers touched the flag-covered bier. I felt the coffin move, and my heart jumped.

And then I realized that the coffin was unsteady, and that each mourner who bent to pat or kiss it made it stir just a little, rocking it softly, as if to aid his rest.

SYLVAN MEYER
THE DAILY TIMES, GAINESVILLE, LA.
June 6, 1968

What good is it to call the Robert Kennedy shooting a tragedy, or to deplore violence or to bemoan the nation's directions? Perhaps the good is to awaken people to the costs of violence, to alarm those who speak in extremes of threats and warnings, who attack motives and individuals rather than their ideas. The irresponsible writer and speaker today, in a violent time, holds the gun at the country's head.

I thought, quite naturally, of Bob Kennedy the man rather than Kennedy the politician-image, when the jolting news came through the immediate and intimate TV screen. Kennedy evoked either great respect and loyalty or intense hostility. I could never see the basis for the hostility, although I could understand why people disagreed with him.

Kennedy personified the efficient, red-tape slashing, direct executive. He drew his own goals clearly and expressed them well. Not nearly so liberal as his political opponents painted him, he looked for methods that would make goals attainable in our time. He disliked waste or bumbling.

I could never understand the ruthless label. He merely made himself crystal clear and so probably hurt some feelings. But you do not consider a man ruthless when you enjoy a breakfast with him on the terrace of his home, watch his byplay with his children and his dogs and see him wipe some stray shaving cream from his ears as he comes downstairs to greet friends.

Around him, Kennedy gathered men of tremendous dedication to America: decorated war heroes, newsmen of unquestioned integrity and unimpeachable convictions about the worth and future of this country; learned men willing to submerge their own careers in service, not to Kennedy, but to this nation.

Among them and between them and Kennedy there was an electric crackle of ideas and plans. Yet, in my few, brief contacts with them, not as an insider by any means, I never heard a selfish motive expressed nor any concept of gain or advantage for any person, area or private goal.

God forbid that any more martyrs to human kindness and governmental justice are created in this country. We are already burdened with losses of intellect, courage and leadership that have subtracted immeasurably from America's assets.

Can we have reason again in our dealings with each other?

THEODORE C. SORENSEN
THE SATURDAY REVIEW
June 22, 1968

To begin with, Robert Kennedy is dead. No words can alter that unalterable fact. No tears can console our inconsolable grief, and no monument or memorial can replace that irreplaceable figure whose leadership and laughter and love of fellow man are now lost.

Thus it is hard for those of us who loved and looked to him to expose our wounds with words before time has crusted them over just a little. But much of what *is* being spoken and written today revolves around Robert Kennedy's death; and we shall only be multiplying the tragedy of that mindless, senseless act if *our* memories do not revolve around his life.

It is not his death but his life that speaks volumes against the folly and futility of violence. If his spirit now cries out to us to halt, it calls upon us to halt not merely the unlimited sale of guns, but the unlimited killing of men, whether it is done in defiance of the law or in the name of the law, by the assassin or by a nation. And to urge in his name repressive anti-crime legislation which he opposed is to turn tragedy into travesty.

Oh yes, much will be said and written about his death. Let *us* honor and remember his life. It was a beautiful life—so unfairly brief but so incredibly full, marked by sorrow but overflowing with joy, too short to do all that he wanted to do, but long enough to leave more lasting legacies to all mankind than a legion of lesser men could have achieved at twice his age. It was a meaningful life—blessed with the love of a wonderful wife and children, enriched by the shining example of a brother whom he loved and served and helped make great, and preserved in masterful books and speeches and pieces of legislation that rightly bear his name.

And yet, for such a public man, it was a surprisingly private life. He was adored by millions, excoriated by thousands, but known, truly known, by very, very few. Those who saw only the toughness of his hide could not have believed the tenderness of his heart. Those who marveled at the majesty of his public presence could not have understood the modesty of his private thoughts. It would surprise those critics who spoke so stupidly about his ruthlessness to know that in fact, in the poet's words, "His life was *so* gentle, and the elements *so* mixed in him, that nature might stand on its feet and say to all the world: this was a man." Perhaps it is fitting that his final passing came in the Hospital of the Good Samaritan, named for another man whose compassion and mercy were unknown to his detractors.

Even some of his friends helped to blur the picture. Because his foes tried to picture him as tough, ambitious and relentless, we tried to say that he was not, but he was—tough enough to withstand those slings and arrows of misfortune and malice that have driven other men from the field, ambitious enough to increase his contribution to his country, and relentless in his pursuit of justice for all and hopelessness for none. They said he took advantage of the fact that he was a Kennedy. And indeed he did, using his father's private wealth to do public good, turning his mother's religious teachings into practical deeds and translating his brother's golden legacy into an explicit charter of hope.

Unlike his brother, Robert Kennedy never became President of the United States—although I truly believe he was on his way to becoming one of the greatest—but he molded more minds and inspired more hearts in this and other nations than nearly all of the men who served in that exalted post. Like his brother, he forsook comfort for country, grew wiser and warmer as he grew older, preferred candor to clichés in both formal and informal utterances, laughed at himself more often than at others, forgave even those who reviled him, and was struck down by the assassin's bullet at the height of his power and glory.

There is no curse upon the Kennedys. They have more than their share of ill-fate because they had more than their share of the courage and the conviction required to dare and to try and to tempt fate. They believed with Sir Francis Bacon that there is no comparison between that which is lost by not succeeding and that which is lost by not trying. They died heroic deaths because they lived heroic lives.

Those lives were not wasted. The bitterness of our anguish today cannot cause us to forget the lasting value of their valiant labors. An so it is that we remember now, especially now, how Robert Kennedy appeared before the Democratic National Convention's memorial service for his brother in 1964 and recited these words from Shakespeare:

> ...when he shall die
> Take him and cut him out in little stars
> And he shall make the face of heaven so fine
> That all the world will be in love with night....

JAMES THOMAS JACKSON
WATTS WRITERS' WORKSHOP
LOS ANGELES UNDERGROUND

We talked to this cat like he was a soul brother going astray. Like we were all off on a tangent or something. He sat there in Harry Dolan's cramped office, in Harry's Buddha-like chair, in this ghettoed house turned dormitory, turned school for black writers. He interlaced his fingers and listened to us writers-to-be blow our minds and possibly his.

I told him he was a "boss cat" and that we dug his brother, also. I remember Vallejo Ryan Kennedy, one of our young poets, asking him a very curious question: "What street did you come down?" At first I didn't get Vallejo's point and the Senator didn't either. The Senator looked at him curiously. Then it dawned on me. And the Senator also. Because Vallejo was merely asking him if he had come down the main drag where everything was spit and polish as befits a person of his stature, garlanded with roses, the usual protocol bull, or did he actually, ride *through* the ghetto. It was confirmed that he had done both. Then, I said to myself, he had come through Charcoal Alley which is ever garlanded with the good, the bad, and the ugly. He answered mildly yes, he had come that way too. That he had wanted to see Watts in the flesh and some of the things that we had been bitching about since the August revolt of 1965 that had been manifested to him were more or less true and correct. I felt from the way he answered us the possibility existed that he could be interested in our cause.

Budd Schulberg was there. A couple of other Senators, Clark and Murphy, I think. And some dudes that might have been security guards or something. Anyway, they were awfully quiet and they should have been because we were mad as hell and it was our time to bitch anyway. So, for an hour and a half we sat there and shot the breeze, talking to this man about things that sorely needed talking about.

We batted things around a bit. What was this writer's workshop? What was this bit with Watts? Did the people know what they really wanted? And were we the ones to explain it? He had heard that our strange, never before heard of black organization, making so much noise to the written words of poetry, novels, plays, our television programs, Losers Weepers, Jeepers Creepers, and all the rest that he had to see for himself. He convinced us that we were a novelty to him and his entourage, was convinced also and showed it in their expressions. They were quiet as mice when the cat's about and didn't interrupt us at all. After all, this young bloke with a tousled forelock was having his day at our place, but in our groove, in our time, in our way. God knows we had gone their way—the villains—long enough. But, he was listening. And he was concerned. Groovy, babe.

How were we to know that this brash young man would reappear twice more to our establishment and in Watts period, helping to champion our causes and in the doing making him dear to our hearts, keeping him ever gentle on our minds.

He wasn't a bad dude. He spoke well, articulate, eloquent, the average American digs a family. Man, this cat was boss family—ten crumb crushers and one more on the way makes us think that he was taking care of business—and that makes for a good dude, fully acceptable in our society. For whatever that's worth.

This dude that shot him—who is he—who was he? What possible aims could he have had in killing this young valiant out to fight our present wars? So, with the death of a hero we gain an anti-hero, a nonentity and an unknowledgeable bastard and the world is worse off for its loss.

This is a salute, a praise, a benediction, a farewell; this is a letter to a soul going home; this is to a not so bad dude who took the time and the patience to sit and listen to a few would be writers at Douglass House those few moons ago when he came down our street, Charcoal Alley and vowed to do something about our li'l old problems. This is forever, eternal, everlasting unto everlasting. I will miss you, baby. This is not the end of life, not the end of Douglass House. You came down our street, Charcoal Alley; white folks, black folks, people who dug you and your fabulous brother. We feel that we had something, somehow in common and you weren't such a bad dude after all.

ARTHUR SCHLESINGER, JR.
THE WASHINGTON POST AND THE LOS ANGELES TIMES
June 9, 1968

No one ever forgot, of course, that Robert Kennedy was the brother of a President of the United States, and some accused him of running for the Presidency on his brother's coattails. Yet Robert Kennedy had not only an identity and a record which would have entitled him to consideration for the Presidency had none of his relatives even been elected to anything higher than city assemblymen.

This record began in a serious sense when, amid almost total skepticism on Capitol Hill and among the press, John Kennedy appointed Robert Kennedy his Attorney General. Skepticism was understandable. Robert Kennedy was hardly 35. His legal experience had been limited to service as counsel for senatorial committees, and there his role had been one of a zealous—many thought overzealous—prosecutor.

His chief fame then was as the manager of his brother's campaign. His designation as the Nation's chief law enforcement officer seemed an act of dynastic indulgence. Why not, someone said, make him Postmaster General, like Jim Farley?

But Robert Kennedy was a good deal more than a party manager. His brother valued his intelligence and judgment and wanted him by his side. They had thought for a moment of a deputy or assistant secretaryship—perhaps in Defense or in Latin American affairs at State—but their father had pointed out this would put the official who stood between the brother and the President in an impossible position.

So the President-elect decided to go ahead with the Attorney Generalship. He later told Ben Bradlee how he planned to announce the appointment: "I think I'll open the front door of the Georgetown house some morning about two A.M., look up and down the street and, if there's no one there, I'll whisper, 'It's Bobby.'"

When the moment finally came, and the brothers started out the door to face the press, he said, "Damn it, Bobby, comb your hair." We were still saying that seven and one-half years later.

As Attorney General, Kennedy was plunged into the heart of the racial crisis. He came to this crisis with strong general sympathies but without much specific background, and he learned very quickly. He learned above all of the determination of his black fellow citizens to achieve their rights. He believed in the justice of their cause and respected their courage, and his own exceptional feeling for the excluded groups, his curious sense of identification with the casualties and victims of American society, gave him the power to command the confidence of those who had no one to trust.

He called out the troops to put James Meredith into the University of Mississippi. He managed the passage of sweeping civil rights legislation. And his concern extended to the poor in general, especially through his Committee on Juvenile Delinquency, which originated many of the ideas and programs later carried forward in the war against poverty.

His relationship to his brother, moreover, meant his involvement in a far wider range of public questions than any other Attorney General in our history. He did not take part in the meetings which preceded the Bay of Pigs, but thereafter President Kennedy took no crucial decision in foreign policy without making sure that Robert Kennedy was there.

Next to the President, Robert Kennedy played the most important role in the peaceful resolution of the Cuban missile crisis. At the start, he led the opposition to the proposal that we take out the missile bases by surprise air attack and, at the end, when two messages of different import arrived from Khrushchev, he conceived the idea of ignoring the second and harsher message and responding to the more reasonable negotiating terms set forth in the first.

Beyond all this, Robert Kennedy was, in effect, the nerve center of the New Frontier. Every New Frontiersman, chopping his way through the thickets of Government, tended to turn to Robert Kennedy when he encountered obstacles and frustrations. The Attorney General had a sort of roving mandate through the Government, and he used it with discretion and imagination to reinforce liberal ideas and initiatives on matters from the release of Junius Scales to our policy in Africa, Latin America, and Indonesia.

There was a tendency to feel that Robert Kennedy as a Senator was more liberal than he had been as Attorney General and to attribute this to his New York constituency. This was not so. The effect of Dallas was not to transform his convictions but to give them a new dimension and quality. His brother's murder intensified his own sense of the awful fortuity of life.

He now inclined more than ever toward that fatalism which saw human existence in terms of a tragic destiny but did not relieve man from his obligation to strive as best he could for the right. He found comfort in Aeschylus and also in Camus, and he evolved for himself a personal faith, a kind of Catholic stoicism and existentialism.

Elective politics also developed latent qualities in what had been a somewhat abstracted and diffident man. He became, for example, an excellent speaker, and he was at his best when he went among the poor and the helpless, whether in hospitals or Indian reservations, in hovels along the Mississippi delta or in the teeming ghettos of New York or Los Angeles. These years strengthened his sense of identification with the untouchables of American society. He made himself in the Senate the particular champion of those who in the past had been the constituents of no one. He was the representative of the unrepresented.

This made the fashionable complaint of 1968 that he was a divisive figure so irrelevant. No doubt he was divisive in the country clubs and the manufacturers' associations. But in the context of the great and terrible divisions of American society—affluent America vs. destitute America, white America vs. black America—he was the most unifying figure in our politics. No one else offered such a possibility of a bridge between the alienated groups and the official American community.

He continued his fight, of course, for restraint and rationality in foreign affairs, and he spoke out against military escalation in Vietnam as early as the spring of 1965—long before any other of the current presidential aspirants.

It was an intense sorrow for him that his hesitation in entering the presidential competition of 1968 lost him the support of so many among the young and in the intellectual community; these he regarded as his natural constituency. But I have no doubt that after California and South Dakota he could have been well on his way to regaining their confidence and backing.

He was a brilliant and devoted man, superbly equipped by intelligence, judgment and passion for the great tasks of national leadership. He was, indeed, better prepared for the Presidency than his brother had been in 1960. His experience had been wider, and he had been exposed to more of the terrible problems of his own country and the world. He was, I deeply believe, our nation's most promising leader.

In his private relations, he was a man of exceptional gentleness and generosity—the best of husbands and fathers, the dearest of friends. He was, in addition, a man of the most irresistible and rueful wit. I spent Thursday, May 30, with him as he whistle-stopped through the Central Valley of California. What lingers in memory are the faces of the crowd, worn and tired faces, weathered in the sun, lighting into a kind of happy hope as he appeared on the back platform of the train and launched into that characteristic combination of banter and intensity with which he beguiled and exhorted his audiences.

He went through this all with his sense of fatality. Perhaps no one would have been less surprised than Robert Kennedy himself by the tragic conclusion of his life. He was vividly aware of the interior tensions of American society; that is why he mingled his attack on social and racial injustice with insistence on the defense of the peaceful processes of change. He loved his fellow citizens and was prepared to trust himself to them, and the quality of his love was such that it would surely have survived the depraved and terrifying act that destroyed him.

Just two months earlier, he had stood at dusk on a street corner in Indianapolis, his voice breaking with emotion, telling a black audience that the Reverend Dr. Martin Luther King, Jr. had been murdered. He said, "In this difficult time for the United States, it is perhaps well to ask what kind of a nation we are." Black people, he said, might understandably be "filled with bitterness, with hatred, and a desire for revenge." We can move in that direction as a country, he said. "Or we can make an effort, as Martin Luther

King did, to understand and to comprehend, and to replace that violence, that stain of bloodshed that has spread across our land, with an effort to understand with compassion and love."

That stain of bloodshed is now deeper than ever. With the murder of Robert Kennedy, following on the murder of John Kennedy and the murder of Martin Luther King, we have killed the three great embodiments of our national idealism in this generation. Each murder had brought us one stage further in the downward spiral of moral degradation and social disintegration. "What we need in the United States," Robert Kennedy said that sad spring evening in Indianapolis, "is not violence or lawlessness, but love and wisdom, and compassion toward one another and a feeling of justice toward those who still suffer within our country."

JAMES WHITTAKER
EULOGY

As Kennedy Campaign Chairman for the State of Washington, and personal friend of Senator Kennedy, I am honored to speak for all the people here who worked for him, loved and admired him, and for those that mourn what the family and friends have lost, and what the country and the world have lost.

He had a good life. He loved it completely and he lived it intensely. He poured so much life into a single day, and he was always learning. On Mt. Kennedy in the Yukon in four days' time he became a qualified mountaineer, learned the history of climbing, of Sherpa life in the Himalayas, and learned even more about those of us with whom he climbed.

So we became friends.

Back in Washington in the Senate, at Hickory Hill with guests, with the children at touch football, or during long evening discussions, he encouraged, stimulated, and challenged. In the rapids of the Salmon River or drifting down the Colorado, skiing at Sun Valley or paddling down the Hudson, my wife and children watched the magic of Bob Kennedy and we grew to love him.

He was so many things to so many people, as well as a gifted, natural leader. He gave inspiration and hope to those of us who knew him, and even to those who did not. He would stand up and say, as he did in a speech in South Africa: "There is discrimination in this world, and slavery, and slaughter, and starvation. A Government represses their people and millions are trapped in poverty while the nation grows rich and wealth is lavished on armaments everywhere." And then he would rededicate himself to what the Greeks wrote so many years ago "to tame the savageness of man and make gentle the life of the world," and so he moved to help the disadvantaged, to right the wrongs, to stop the suffering.

As he moved to seek the newer world he said "each time a man stands up for an ideal, or goes to improve the lot of others or strikes out against injustice, he sends forth a tiny ripple of hope, and crossing each other from a million different centers of energy and power those ripples build a current that can sweep down the mightiest walls of oppression and resistance." This was the man. He continued to seek, to strive, and not to yield.

The night of the California Primary a few of the Kennedy people met with a number of uncommitted delegates in the Presidential Suite of the Olympic Hotel. The TV sets were on and there was gay exuberance as the primary results came in. A speaker was hooked up to a telephone to broadcast the voice of Senator Kennedy. At eleven P.M., Senator Kennedy spoke to the audience and asked us to help him seek his goals. I thanked him for the call and said, "Congratulations, Bob, keep up the good work, we love you!"

The next day in the hospital, I knelt by the bed, held his hand and Ethel's hand, and cried for what she had lost, for what those who knew him had lost and for what those that had never known him had lost. I cried for the ones that might never say, "I am a better man because I knew him."

As we flew to New York in Air Force I, I recalled the day in Colorado when we ascended with the children the seven-mile trail out of the Grand Canyon. The temperature was 110° and there was a question of whether we would make it or not. As we rested in the shade Bob quoted from memory:

> This day is called The Feast of Crispian.
> He that outlives this day, and comes safe home,
> Will stand a-tiptoe when this day is named
> And rouse him as the name of Crispian.
> He that shall live this day, and see old age,
> Will yearly on the vigil, feast his neighbours,
> and say "Tomorrow is St. Crispian."
> Then will he strip his sleeve and show his scars,
> And say, "These wounds I had on Crispians Day."
> Old men forget; yet all shall be forgot,
> But he'll remember, with advantages,
> What feats he did that day. Then shall our names,
> Familiar in his mouth as household words—
> Harry the King, Bedford and Exeter, Warwick and Talbot,
>   Salisbury and Gloucester,
> Be in their flowing cups freshly remembered.
> This story shall the good man teach his son;
> And Crispian Crispian shall ne'er go by,
> From this day till the ending of the world,
> But we in it shall be remembered
> We few, we happy few, we band of brothers;
> For he today that sheds his blood today with me
> Shall be my brother, be he ne'er so vile,
> And Gentlemen in England now abed
> Shall think themselves accur'd
> They were not here and
> Hold their manhoods cheap whilst any speaks
> That fought with us upon St. Crispian's Day.

On the train to Arlington, in the last car with the coffin, I heard the voices of the people as we passed. Some were shouting and more were crying. Their voices drifted in over the clatter of the wheels on the track as we rolled through the countryside:

We love you, Bobby

Good-bye, Kennedy

Pray for us, Bobby.

To those of us that knew him, worked for him, loved him and were inspired by him, we must say in Shakespeare's words:

> His life was gentle and the elements so mixed in him that
> Nature might stand on its feet and
> Say to all the world—'This was a man.'

SENATOR GEORGE MCGOVERN

INTRODUCTION OF SENATOR ROBERT F. KENNEDY, SIOUX FALLS AND RAPID CITY, SOUTH DAKOTA

April 16, 1968

For reasons that most of you understand, I have seen fit not to take sides in the current presidential contest for the Democratic nomination. I feel that my fellow South Dakotans should make their own decision.

All three men now being considered as candidates—Senators Kennedy and McCarthy and Vice President Humphrey—are close and treasured friends of mine. Each of them would serve our nation well. Each of them would have my cooperation as President. Each of them knows that situations might develop where I would disagree with him.

And may I add that President Johnson has taken on new stature and dignity by the magnanimous manner in which he placed his view of the Vietnam issue above his desires for re-election.

But I do want to say to my fellow South Dakotans in the presence of our distinguished guest that if he is elected President of the United States, he will, in my judgment, become one of the three or four greatest Presidents in our national history.

I have heard the talk about his ruthlessness and his long hair. But he isn't as ruthless as was the great Theodore Roosevelt, and his hair isn't half as long as Thomas Jefferson's, and unlike Abraham Lincoln, he has no beard at all. What he does have is the absolute personal honesty of a Woodrow Wilson, the stirring passion for leadership of Andrew Jackson, and the profound acquaintance with personal tragedy of Abraham Lincoln.

Recently, one of our nation's most eloquent preachers was slain at Memphis. In one of his finest sermons, he took for his text the words of the Great Teacher: "Be ye therefore wise as serpents and harmless as doves."

"We must," said Dr. King, "combine the toughness of the serpent and the softness of the dove, a tough mind and a tender heart."

One of the reasons, I suspect, that some people are puzzled by Senator Kennedy is that he is a tough-minded man with a tender heart. He is, to borrow Dr. King's fitting description of the good life, "a creative synthesis of opposites."

The Presidency is a sobering office that calls forth the seeds of greatness. Many a man whose talents were undetected or misinterpreted took on new stature in the White House. I think that was true of the late John F. Kennedy who became a greater man with each passing month he lived in the presidential office.

You people know the affection and the esteem I held for President Kennedy, but it is my carefully measured conviction that Senator Robert Kennedy, even more than our late beloved President, would now bring to the Presidency a deeper measure of experience and a more profound capacity to lead our troubled land into the light of a new day.

So while I decline to endorse any presidential candidate prior to the national convention, I do speak from the heart about a gallant friend and colleague whom I now present with pride to you—Senator Robert Kennedy.

SENATOR JACOB JAVITS
EULOGY
July 30, 1968

Mr. President, first, may I express my gratitude to the majority leader for giving me what I consider to be a great privilege to begin this Senate eulogy today.

Senator Kennedy was not just my colleague, although that alone would be all that would be required to make me say what I am about to say. But in the course of our association, which naturally became much more intimate when he became a Senator, he became my friend.

His hope and idealism made him a force for constructive change which inspired the youth of the Nation. He had, so far as I know, the deepest concern for the underdog of anyone I had ever met. To put it in very blunt terms, he had deep concern for the people whom our society—notwithstanding its many blessings, and it does have them—had disfranchised in terms of opportunity and in terms of the legacy to which we feel all Americans are entitled. He was not the only man in public life to have this feeling in his heart; but, in my judgment, it burned in him more brightly than in any other man I have ever known.

He had great humor and wit. He did not take himself all that seriously. But when his mind directed itself to this problem, he throbbed with its significance, like an Old Testament prophet. This was his prophecy: that the blessings of American life would be transmitted to all Americans; to the poor, the black, the Mexican-American, the Japanese-American, and other hyphenated Americans—hyphenated only because they lagged so seriously behind the condition of other Americans and because they were oppressed rather than uplifted by the society of which we are all a common part.

Senator Kennedy had a keen understanding that 80 percent or more of American society was enjoying a way of life, a freedom, a health, an amplitude of living which had never been vouchsafed to any people in all of recorded history. His deep feeling and his burning zeal for improvement came notwithstanding the fact that the disinherited were a minority—20 percent or less—of the Nation.

It was this deep feeling which transmuted our relationship from one of colleagues working together in the interests of our State, to one of friends.

Mr. President, Senator Kennedy's passion for the integrity and the quality of our society and for justice, especially for the oppressed, was coupled with one other deep conviction—his insistence that what was done about it should be done in such a way as to preserve—or to confer, where it did not exist—the dignity of the individual. This is where his deep heritage as a Catholic and as a religious man—and he was that—became evident.

His passion for improvement and his passion of sympathy for the oppressed and the depressed was joined with the determination that every man had a spark of the divine, was king in his own right. He was determined that whatever was done about the condition of these people, they could never be patronized but should be given the opportunity to stand up and help themselves as individuals of dignity. These twin ideas so fired and infused his personality that he became a flaming symbol of hope and of idealism and a tremendous medium for constructive change for the people of our Nation, particularly for the young, whose hearts went out to him almost without his uttering a word.

I should like to recount a few of our joint undertakings which reflected the tremendous feeling that impressed me so very deeply. I recall, for example, that it was my colleague who, in the first months in the Senate, suggested that a number of counties in the southern tier of our State of New York—a wealthy State by general standards, but with pockets of difficulty in poverty, as we all know—be included in the program for Appalachia. He started it; he thought it up. He saw the reality, and he saw where it fitted geographically and economically. Again, this was the first expression that he was able to give vent to here of this deep sympathy for the oppressed and depressed. The citizens of that region, in my judgment, have benefitted greatly from this association, and I hope they will always have a very dear spot in their hearts for Senator Kennedy. I joined him in the effort, but I am the first to say that he espoused it, developed it, and made it come to fruition.

Another effort in which we both joined was to allow those persons from Puerto Rico who had graduated from Spanish-language schools on the island to vote without taking a literacy test in English. This provided an easier transition and allowed them to vote without a feeling of inhibition that their status as Americans changed because they moved from Puerto Rico to the mainland. This act is a tremendous achievement. We were again partners in this effort. This memory of his concern will live in the hearts of tens of thousands of Puerto Rican citizens of the United States now living on the mainland.

Mr. President, there are two other instances. Probably the most deeply felt for both of us occurred at Jackson, Miss., and in the communities that surround it. Here we encountered, first in the hearings, and later physically and directly, in fact that there was starvation in our country, or such malnutrition as to be equivalent to starvation. This was a horrendous fact and the repercussions of it have not yet ended.

It will be recalled that even since the tragic assassination of Senator Kennedy we have had debates in this Chamber dealing with the effort to make money available to deal with emergency conditions of malnutrition amounting to starvation. But the reaction to these personal visual evidences of what it meant to be depressed in this country left Senator Kennedy practically shaking with indignation, and he never ceased to declaim against what he considered to be one of the worst inequities that his work in the Senate had uncovered.

Together with the Senator from Pennsylvania (Mr. Clark) and myself, he endured personal mental torture in the feeling that we were all commonly guilty when such conditions could exist in our country.

He was a strong advocate of help for handicapped children. It was his deep feeling that rehabilitation would give them dignity and nobility and purpose rather than purposelessness and depression because of their affliction.

In terms of human dignity, it is known that he was an ardent proponent of allowing the poor to be relieved of the demeaning means test and caseworker investigations which have so characterized and bedeviled all welfare programs. He cried out against it. His indignation and the case he made will be a landmark for the improvements which we are now making and which we will make in the years ahead.

One of his most signal achievements was a very gifted program in Brooklyn. For this project, he called into partnership with him the mayor of New York, John Lindsay, and me. But on his own he went into the reconstruction of life in a slum area, the Bedford-Stuyvesant section of Brooklyn. He called on the techniques of government and business cooperation, which he had the privilege to develop, and which was probably the greatest bond in the cement between us. His plan had the understanding of our committee chairman, the Senator from Alabama (Mr. Hill), and Members such as the Senator from Oregon (Mr. Morse) and the Senator from Texas (Mr. Yarborough), and the great leadership of the chairman of our subcommittee, the Senator from Pennsylvania (Mr. Clark).

In the Bedford-Stuyvesant effort he literally created out of the ground the machinery for community cooperation and a most gifted and high-level board of directors and some leading businessmen, bankers, and community leaders of New York. It was said the board of directors was almost overwhelming considering the size of the project involved, and with its prestige would have been an excellent board for a countrywide effort of the same character. I know that he put this plan together personally through dozens of telephone calls and visits which elicited help from most of the distinguished people of our city.

His effort will be a landmark of self-help and, in my judgment, it will help to rebuild that entire area occupied by 600,000 people living in the most depressed circumstances in slum conditions, as bad as anyone could find in any big city. I am confident the area will be reconstructed and that it will be the most noble monument which could be erected to his deep feeling for the depressed, to his passion for constructive change, and to the determination that it shall all be done to preserve and fortify the dignity of the individual.

I am pleased to report to the Senate that his wonderfully gracious and heroic wife, Ethel Kennedy, has agreed to serve on the board of directors of the Bedford-Stuyvesant project, of which I am also privileged to be a member.

Mr. President, I close by saying that much of what Senator Kennedy believed in, much of the passion that filled his life, will survive. He was a man of action. And his feeling for action has been translated not only into legislation and reality of a Bedford-Stuyvesant project, and other projects, but also into the hearts and minds of millions of Americans. As I said some time ago to a group of young workers who were starting out on a school project in New York, the way they can add 10 percent to everything they do is to feel they are doing it in the memory of Senator Kennedy.

His influence will continue. There is work to be done. We must make provision to provide a balanced diet to the many, many Americans, perhaps in the millions, who are suffering from malnutrition in this country. We must provide the opportunity for all our citizens to train for meaningful work and occupy meaningful jobs, to revamp our welfare laws to give the unfortunate an opportunity to work their way out of hardship with dignity and respect. To provide meaningful firearms control laws which will enable communities, especially slum communities, to live with some sense of order and tranquility—at least to try to do so without the added threat which armed crime brings.

In all of these causes, Mr. President, I will feel personally sustained and inspired—and so will millions of Americans—because they were causes that Robert Kennedy espoused with personal dedication.

This feeling, this concept of alleviating human distress and establishing a dignity of the individual, is truly the touchstone of Robert Kennedy's life.

It should be the touchstone of our actions here as the greatest memorial that we could erect for the Senator.

I still start, every once in a while, as I sit at my desk, and look over my shoulder when the door opens and closes rather quickly, as this was his way of entering this Chamber. I still think sometimes that I shall hear, "Good morning, Senator. What's doing today?" For this used to be Robert Kennedy's little charade with me, suddenly to appear behind me and call me "Senator," although we knew each other well.

I hope it may ever be so, for myself and my colleagues, and for millions of other Americans. That spritely step, that quick smile, that witty word, and that deep dedication and earnest feeling of zeal for the underdog could serve no better purpose than to animate us and animate the country and have a profound influence upon our destiny.

Mr. President, I again thank the majority leader for the signal honor he has accorded me in allowing me to be the first to pay tribute to Senator Robert Kennedy this morning.

SENATOR ABRAHAM RIBICOFF
EULOGY
July 30, 1968

Mr. President, we mourn the loss of Robert F. Kennedy, a close colleague and a warm friend.

The horror of the tragedy is with us, though many weeks have gone by. The full magnitude of our loss endures, despite the passage of time.

For a devoted family and loving friends are now denied the counsel and courage, inspiration, love, and trust that filled the proud example Robert Kennedy set.

Perhaps it is the most telling measure of the man that millions in our nation and the world feel a keen personal loss, like those of us who knew him well.

In the cities and villages of Latin America where he went, in the towns and capitals of both Western and Eastern Europe and South Africa, men, great and small, are grieved.

And so it is at home—where people of all ages, colors, and creeds across the country join in sorrow with the people of the State he represented well. For Bob Kennedy cared about people. They knew this because of his efforts to help improve their lives.

He held up the wrongs of our nation, and he worked to make them right. He aroused men to put forth their best efforts to correct the injustices of our land, and he awakened them to the infinite possibilities of life for all mankind.

Bob Kennedy looked into history and drew the important lesson that short-sighted living brings long regrets. From there he set out to do what he thought he must to help conquer hunger, poverty, war, and assaults on human dignity—the enemies of men.

Bob Kennedy had a passion in life. It was to create a society where every American can fulfill his potential, and where no American is held back by race or color or for want of the opportunity to succeed.

Young people flocked to his side not only because he was a young, attractive, vital man himself. They were drawn by his youthful spirit—a remarkable blend of warmth, idealism, and faith. He challenged them and they took up the challenge. For he made them understand that their future depends on the present that all of us share.

Robert Kennedy was a thoughtful, wise, and considerate man. I came to know him well in 1956 when we worked closely together while seeking the Vice Presidency for his brother, John F. Kennedy. Our relationship was maintained from 1956 through 1960, during our efforts to win the presidential nomination for his brother.

Robert Kennedy was devoted to his brother. We came to the Cabinet together in 1961, and I was deeply impressed by the dedication and distinction with which he served the President and our country. As Attorney General, he not only led the Department of Justice with courage and conviction—he also lent his abilities and judgment to some of the most crucial decisions this country faced.

After the tragic death of the President, Robert Kennedy became a Senator from the State of New York. In the Senate we served together on the Subcommittee on Executive Reorganization. Again we worked closely together, this time in the fields of traffic safety, urban problems, and the problems of rising health costs.

There has always been a warm and special feeling between the Kennedy family and the people of Connecticut. We have grown to know them well. They have been our neighbors and our frequent guests.

Now we share their grief, for in the death of Senator Robert Kennedy we have seen repeated the terrible tragedy that took President John F. Kennedy away from us.

Their leadership—their voices, vitality, and spirit—are sorely missed. Our loss will always be remembered and often recalled.

Robert Kennedy, and his brother before him, led lives that were far too brief. But they left behind them meaningful monuments that make ours a better nation and world.

It is our task to carry on.

Robert Kennedy often told us that "we can do better." We have long known the truth of his words. We must act upon them now.

SENATOR WINSTON PROUTY
EULOGY
July 30, 1968

Mr. President, we are today a little further removed in time from the tragic event of June 5, which took from our midst and deprived the world of our late colleague, Robert F. Kennedy. My sense of personal loss and our bereavement as a body and as a nation are no less real now than when I spoke briefly on the sixth of June. If these short two months have done anything, they have intensified my feeling of frustration and helplessness in the face of so senseless an act.

Mr. President, I have thought about the short years that Robert Kennedy was among us in the Senate. I have tried, also, to compare the Senate itself during that time and since his death. There is, indeed, a change in this body. It seems to me that the poignant touch which his very presence added to our assembly was, if not unique, so keen and vigorous as to have given added life to us all.

Of course, we never have agreed and never will agree in all things. And, right or wrong, once decided, our work is done, and we move to other things. But, now our approach is just a shade different, it seems to me.

It was in his approach to things that, I think, Bob Kennedy made his mark. The urgency toward accomplishment which appeared in everything he tried to do was infectious. It seemed to lead us all to be about our business and the business of the nation and to move on to other things.

"We must act," his very presence among us seemed to say. And this approach to things seemed to me to cause our step to quicken, just a little, and to move each of us, however slightly, closer to accomplishment of our goals, whatever they are.

It seemed to me that Robert Kennedy conveyed to us a sense of satisfaction —not that we have done a complete job; not that we have accomplished everything; but a sense of belonging because we are doing something; that the job is being done; that we are acting in a living, vibrant world.

It is this worthwhile motion which has been slowed down. It is in the act of accomplishing things that now we feel most strongly the absence of the junior Senator from New York.

PATRICK J. LUCEY
WISCONSIN STATE DEMOCRATIC CONVENTION
July 19, 1968

Mr. Chairman, Fellow Delegates: I cannot tell you how sorry I am that this convention could not have opened on schedule six weeks ago.

Had an assassin's hand been stayed, Senator Robert Francis Kennedy would have keynoted this convention. Hundreds of thousands of cheering citizens would have lined the streets from Billy Mitchell Field to this banquet hall. A surge of excitement would have passed through a cheering capacity crowd in this room as he rose to speak.

All of you would have shared a sense of participation in the making of history as you did in 1960.

Whatever your own candidate preference, you would have felt the satisfaction of involvement in the making of a President. And as we departed this convention, a scent of victory would have been in the air, and each of us would have felt somehow ennobled by our commitment to a larger purpose.

The magic is gone . . . the demand that we do better is silenced . . . the voice of conscience is stilled. Who is there now to remind us that we are, in fact, our brother's keeper? Who is there to say that this sin of omission is unacceptable, or that condition of hardship among the less fortunate is unsatisfactory? Who will call us to account? Who will remind us of our responsibilities, not just our advantages? Who will take in his hand the black hand of a troubled child in a steaming ghetto, and lead that child into a decent classroom? Who will go to the original concentration camp, the American Indian Reservation, and convince the red-skinned teen-ager that suicide is not the best solution to his problems? Who now can erase the bloody nightmare of Vietnam and make us again worthy of moral leadership on this planet?

Had Robert Francis Kennedy lived, he would have been present at this convention. He would have placed before you the agenda of our nation's unfinished business. He would have insisted that we can do better.

There are those who say his campaign was an exercise in futility, that he could not have won the nomination of our party. But Andrew Jackson once said, "One man with courage makes a majority." No one has ever charged that Robert Francis Kennedy lacked courage.

During the final six months of Senator Kennedy's life, I saw much of him. I stood with him in the ghetto of Indianapolis as he announced to his vast Negro audience that Martin Luther King was dead. I watched and listened as his speech became a prayer, and his audience returned quietly to their homes. I sat before him the next day in Cleveland as he spoke to the City Club of his concern about violence in our society. For five weeks I served his cause in Nebraska, and then moved on to Portland and San Francisco, and finally stood by helplessly that terrible final night in Los Angeles.

Robert Francis Kennedy was probably the most misunderstood man in our society. He was called ruthless ... but few remember that this label was first applied by James Hoffa.

Many resented his appointment by President Kennedy as Attorney General, but as he left that office, the Washington *Post* summed up his record as follows:

"He has guided more important legislation through Congress than did any of his predecessors in the past thirty years. He has made the Federal Government, for the first time, a vigorous enemy of organized crime. He has pushed equal rights for all Americans."

In one of Dr. King's finest sermons, he helped to explain the lack of understanding of the personality of Robert Kennedy. Dr. King suggested that "we must combine the toughness of the serpent and the softness of the dove, a tough mind and a tender heart." Robert Kennedy was of tender heart. He was a man of great compassion. He was at the same time tough-minded, exacting, impatient of slothfulness.

In an introduction of Robert Kennedy in South Dakota, April 16, Senator George McGovern told his audience:

"You people know the affection and esteem I held for President Kennedy, but it is my carefully measured conviction that Senator Robert Kennedy, even more than our beloved President, would now bring to the Presidency a deeper measure of experience and a more profound capacity to lead our troubled land into the light of a new day."

In the same speech, Senator McGovern said of Senator Kennedy that he would "become one of the three or four greatest Presidents in our history."

Many of us found it difficult to put aside the grief that followed the death of President Kennedy, but at least to him it was given to chart his course ... to lay before us his clearly defined goals. Robert Kennedy's plans were just beginning to unfold. His programs were still to be outlined. His potential was just beginning to reach the people.

Perhaps the one occasion when millions of Americans found it easiest to identify with Robert Kennedy was four years ago as he stood briefly before the delegates to the National Convention, and a national television audience, to introduce a film about his brother. For that occasion he chose a passage from Shakespeare's *Romeo and Juliet:*

> And, when he shall die
> Take him and cut him out in little stars
> And he will make the face of heaven so fine
> That all the world will be in love with night
> And pay no worship to the garish sun

As I stood at Arlington in November 1963, I stood again in June, 1968 . . . to see Robert Francis Kennedy buried at his brother's side. And as we read on in *Romeo and Juliet,* we find these lines:

> "Then, dreadful trumpet, sound the general doom!
> For who is living, if those two are gone?"

It would be easy to step aside . . . to say all is lost . . . to abandon hope. But such an act of cowardice would hardly be a fitting tribute to a man of compassion, conviction, and courage.

Our children can live in a better world because Robert Francis Kennedy had a dream, and the courage to try . . . but theirs will be a better world only if we accept with President John Kennedy "that here on earth, God's work must truly be our own."

Come, my friends, 'tis still not too late to seek a newer world.

THE HONORABLE W. AVERELL HARRIMAN
EULOGY

Senator Robert F. Kennedy was one of the most gallant men I have ever known. He was fearless. He faced facts squarely. It was impossible for him not to tell the truth as he saw it. I think that is why some people thought he was ruthless. At times the truth is ruthless. He supported the causes he believed in regardless of the enemies he knew that he would make. But few men have won the deep respect and affection of so many. Negroes and other minorities knew that he had accepted their cause as his own.

If he had been elected President, he would have been a great President. He shared with President Kennedy many of his inspired decisions. He understood the problems of our time, and in some capacity he would have played a major role in forwarding the greatness of our country in which he had such deep faith. Our country has suffered an irreparable loss.

HAROLD MACMILLAN
BBC BROADCAST
June 6, 1968

I always thought Bobby very shy really. Many people thought he was more of a politician than his brother. Many people thought he was, perhaps, a pretty tough politician. So he was. He had the steel; he had the toughness. But he had a curious kind of shyness too. And he—I think like all men who are any good at it—he had a sensitiveness, a very quick feeling about other people. But whatever people may say and whatever history may write about Bobby, he had a genuine compassion—a real love of people, humble people, poor people—I think the word now is underprivileged people. Not [in] a pompous or pedantic ... way ... but genuine. And I think a great deal of that came because he had, as they all had, a real belief that we are God's children and that we must do His work.

ANDREI VOZNESENSKY

TRANSLATED BY WILLIAM JAY SMITH
AND NICHOLAS FERSEN

JUNE '68

Wild swans, wild swans, wild swans,
Northward, northward bound.
Kennedy... Kennedy... the heart
Breaks at the sound.

Of foreign politics
Not much may be understood;
But I do understand

A white cheek bathed with blood.
The idol of TV screens
In his funereal auto rides...
With bullets, bullets, bullets
Madmen proselytize.

When absently he shook
That head while yet intact
I thought of Yesenin
With his tumbling forelock:

As on that poet's brow
A sickle-moon would brood—
For public effect, they thought,
But it proved to be for blood.

How defenseless the challenger,
Politician or poet,
When he topples to gunshot
Right through the TV set!

Oh, the roots of apple trees
Torn from orchard soil,
Mourn high on her balcony
There on the thirtieth floor!

Apple trees, apple trees...
Curse those bloody trees!

Let skyscraper-apples grieve,
Good but to guard a grave.

Note: Voznesensky refers to apple trees that he remembers having seen on the balcony of Mrs. John F. Kennedy's Fifth Avenue apartment, which is on the fifteenth rather than the thirtieth floor; Sergei Yesenin, famous Soviet lyric poet, committed suicide in 1925 at the age of thirty.

CHARLES EVERS
LOOK SPECIAL EDITION
June 1968

He was my brother. There was nothing I wouldn't do for him. There was nothing he wouldn't do for me. We could argue by the hour, to the point of almost cussing. We could communicate in a kind of shorthand—a word here, a word there, a grunt, a nod. Or we could talk to each other with silence, just sitting, sometimes in tears over our shared griefs and frustrations.

At Dr. Martin Luther King's funeral, we both were quite shaken. He comforted me. As we walked together, he said, "Charles, you've got to be more careful." I said, "You've got to be more careful too. We're the only two left. But how can we be careful? Look at all these people here. Any one of them..."

We were the only two left. There were only five of us in the beginning —his brother Jack, my brother Medgar, Dr. King, Bob, and I. Now there is only one.

Who is there to take Bob's place? I don't know. But there must be someone. I can't believe that God would take him from us and not have someone somewhere to replace him.

He was so right for the civil rights movement. He was one of the few men we felt had the touch and the feeling. He really understood what it was all about. He knew that we had to eliminate the cause of movements like ours, that if the people were given a chance, there would be no need to march, to demonstrate, to go to jail in order to have the opportunity to enjoy the things due all of us as human beings and Americans.

It was no accident that the Ku Klux Klan began to crumble while Robert Kennedy was Attorney General. Once he understood the situation, he went after them. And he understood the situation because he had the humility to say, "I don't know," and then to educate himself and, once he knew, to do the right thing.

I remember in 1964, when he was running for the Senate, flying with him from Buffalo to Syracuse. I was AWOL from my job as Mississippi director of the National Association for the Advancement of Colored People, and I was working for him in that campaign, just as I joined him this time. "I admit," he said, "I didn't know too much before about people's cruelty to each other because of color. I knew that it existed, but I didn't realize haw bad it was. When I became Attorney General, I found out. It is very bad."

What made Bob Kennedy different from other politicians was that he meant what he said. You could look in his eyes and at his face and you knew he meant it. He wouldn't just say something nice for his listeners because it was good politics. He was the only one who could feel the pulse of this country. He went on college campuses and told them he was opposed to student deferment from the draft. He went into the worst of the Negro neighborhoods and told the worst of the black militants that he did not like all black people, only some, and that he did not agree with all of their demands, only some. He had the courage to face reality, bitter as it might be, and to make the rest of us face it with him. I know of no man or woman who worked with him who was not elevated in the process, who learned from him to reject the unacceptable and to do better.

Once, long ago, in Jackson, Mississippi, I tested him. Negroes know it is easy to trick white people by agreeing with them, by telling them what they want to hear. We were talking about poverty in Mississippi, and I wanted to try him out and so I said, "Oh, it may not be as bad as some people say." He gave me a sad look and said, "No, Charles, you're wrong. It's worse." He understood.

Another time when we were together, I noticed he had a hole in one of his shoes. He never wore expensive clothes or expensive shoes, just ordinary everyday-looking kinds. But I was surprised by the hole just the same. I laughed and pointed it out to him. "With all your money, how come you've got a hole in your shoe?" I said. He looked, laughed and said, "It's not important. The important thing is that there are millions of people who have holes in their shoes and in their clothes because they can't afford better. In my case, it's pure neglect. Who am I not to have a hole in my shoe?"

He was always a comfort to me. Wherever we were, when he saw me, he would yell out, "Hey, Charles!" Once, he did it in downtown Washington when he was passing by in a car and I was walking. I went to see him about twice a year, and we talked on the phone about once a month. As soon as I got to his office, I could hear him calling, "Let Charles in! Let Charles in!"

Sometimes, we did not do much talking at all. Once, I went to him when there had been so many threats on my life that I did not know what to do, where to turn. We sat in his office and just looked at each other, tears streaming down both our faces. Finally, I told him how discouraged I was, how hopeless it all seemed. "Keep your chin up," he said. "We've got a long way to go." There are times when all a man can do is go to a friend and cry on his shoulder.

He was concerned about people all the time. He cared. When we were talking recently about the make-up of the Mississippi convention delegation, I told him I was working for a delegation that would be loyal to the Democratic party and would include a number of white people as well as Negroes. "Is that good for you, Charles?" he asked. He was concerned because, knowing the past history of Mississippi whites, he felt I might be censured by the Negro community. On one of those last days in California, we picked up a little Negro girl lost in the crowd. As we rode in the open convertible, it became chilly. We were all shivering a little, including Mrs. Kennedy. But his attention was on the girl. "Ethel," he said, "do you have something we can put around her?" But Mrs. Kennedy had nothing, not even for herself. I gave Ethel my coat. He took off his coat, wrapped it around the child and huddled over her. Nobody was around to see. It was just that he cared about people more than about himself.

Robert Kennedy was ruthless, all right. He was ruthless against wrong, against racketeers and hatemongers. He was ruthlessly dedicated to the welfare of all the people. If he had become President, he would have been the President of all the people, but especially of the poor and disadvantaged. We would have seen, during his four or eight years, a change in America that we can hardly conceive of now, a change in the whole atmosphere.

He would have put violence out of our lives. There was no violence at the time of his death and funeral, not a rock thrown, not a window pane broken. In the campaign, he was the only politician with the courage to walk into the toughest ghettos and talk to the black militants. Again, not a boo or a rock thrown. People believed in him. He went to them and talked to them, and they looked at him and listened, and they believed.

When he asked me to help him this time, he said he would understand if I turned him down. The NAACP is nonpartisan, and in 1964, there was some grumbling about my working for him. I told him I did not mind taking the chance of being fired, but I would work only as a volunteer. "You can't pay me," I said. "You can't give me a dime or a million. But I do have a price. My price is that, if you win, you don't forget my people, all the people who are not represented. Do that, and I'll work for you till hell freezes over."

He gave me that sad look. "I won't forget," he said softly. "I want to work for all who are not represented. I want to be their President."

Where, dear God, is the man to take his place?

AMBASSADOR ARTHUR J. GOLDBERG
MEMORIAL SERVICE AT THE HOLY FAMILY CHURCH, NEW YORK CITY
June 9, 1968

It may well be asked why, in a world that contains so much to grieve about, the death of this one individual has struck such a universal chord.

Partly, no doubt, it is because Robert Kennedy had become a world figure, a renowned public servant, and the representative of a family great in leadership, and great also in bravely enduring misfortune—a family to which our prayers and sympathy go out on this day of mourning. His courage and dynamism had captured the imagination of ordinary people the world over. In his death, therefore, countless millions of us felt the sudden loss of a friend, and were reminded of our own mortality. John Donne wrote: "Any man's death diminishes me." The death of this gallant man has diminished us all.

The world was moved and shocked also by the sudden and dreadful manner of his death—so tragically echoing that of his late brother, President John F. Kennedy. The terrible act of assassination all too vividly reminds us that the evils of violence and revenge still lie in men's hearts. We know these violent passions are wholly destructive of the good ends of peace and progress to which all nations and peoples aspire. On this day of mourning for Robert Kennedy, therefore, it is fitting that we resolve anew that men and nations shall forsake the ways of violence and, as the Charter of the Untied Nations bids us all to do, "live together in peace with one another as good neighbors."

Above all, we revere and commemorate Robert Kennedy for the quality of his life. Senator Kennedy was a deeply compassionate man. He was actively concerned over the sufferings and injustices borne by the poor, the deprived and dispossessed, the victims of war, the neglected people of his own America and of the world. He strongly opposed racist doctrines and policies of apartheid in all their forms. For the "newer world" which he advocated, the mere absence of violence was not enough; there must also be the ever-increasing presence of justice, and the ever-growing fulfillment of human rights.

But what is essential, and what Robert Kennedy so splendidly exemplified, is the vibrant belief that these great ideals are not just to be passively wished for, but can actually be realized by the unremitting striving of men. His religious faith was the kind of faith that expressed itself in action. He believed, as his brother President Kennedy said in his famous inaugural address, "that here on earth God's work must truly be our own." And to that belief

Robert Kennedy, like his brother John, gave his abundant courage and vitality all through the days of his short life.

Robert Kennedy was young, not only in his years but in his outlook. He understood well why so many young people today, observing the contrast between their ideals and the reality around them, tend to turn away in discouragement and alienation. By the contagion of his confidence he was able to rally their spirits and restore among them what he called "the sense of possibility."

Now the last page of his life is written, and it is vain to dream of what more this extraordinary young leader might have achieved.

But we who survive will not soon forget the shining example of his short life. He exemplified what was written four centuries ago by Shakespeare's great French contemporary, Montaigne:

> "The advantage of living is not measured by length but by use; some men have lived long, and lived little; attend to it while you are in it. It lies in your will, not in the number of years, for you to have lived enough."

Let us, therefore, so live our lives—be they long or short—that we may help humanity to move toward the newer and better world that Robert Kennedy sought to create. And let us take inspiration from his faith that this age of ours, so full of tragedy and trouble, is also full of excitement and possibility—above all, the possibility of justice and peace and the relief of suffering among the multitudes of the human family.

As His Holiness Pope Paul said in his celebrated address to the United Nations less than three years ago:

> "...brotherly cooperation among the peoples...is what is most beautiful in the United Nations; this is its most truly human face; this is the ideal which mankind dreams of on its pilgrimage through time; this is the world's greatest hope."

Let our memorial to Robert Kennedy and to all the great men who have gone before us, be nothing less than this: our fidelity to that dream and that eternal hope.

Let us in the words of the President's proclamation: "...resolve before God and before each other that the purpose of progress and justice for which Robert F. Kennedy lived shall endure."

U THANT
MEMORIAL SERVICE AT THE HOLY FAMILY CHURCH
June 9, 1968

We are here this afternoon to honor the memory of a gallant public servant brutally cut down in the prime of his life and in the dawn of his fullest promise.

We hope his family may be comforted by the knowledge that the ideas, ideals and achievements of Robert Kennedy will live on and be honored among men everywhere who love peace and justice and who continue the struggle for a better life for all the peoples of the world. But we also know that they have lost a devoted husband, father, son, and brother, a charming and brilliant companion, a man with a rare zest for life, who was the center and inspiration of a wholesome, active and happy circle. He was thoroughly dedicated to public service and the public good and in this service and cause he gave his all. There can be no consolation for such an irreparable loss.

Robert Kennedy, despite his youth and wealth, demonstrated a remarkable ability to communicate with people at all levels. This, I am sure, was because he believed in people, had faith in them and identified with them—and this was clearly sensed by the lowliest, the poor, and the deprived.

Through a senseless act of violence, the world has lost a great and generous spirit. It has lost a man who seemed certain to play, in one way or another, an evermore vital role in the search for solutions to the problems which afflict and bewilder all mankind. Robert Kennedy had already made his mark on history, but he was only at the beginning of his work for peace, for justice, for social progress, for equality and dignity amongst all men, for racial harmony in the United States and elsewhere. He was destined to be a formidable champion in the struggle, to which we are all committed, against poverty, violence, bigotry, and all the conditions that give rise to them. He would have continued to serve as a tireless and resourceful leader in the greatest task which faces us all, the establishment of a civilized and constructive relationship among men and nations. But now he is gone, and we who remain contemplate our loss with sadness and anxiety.

We cannot afford to lose such men. A tragedy of this kind deprives and diminishes us all. Mankind can ill afford to make expendable men of this rare quality.

SENATOR JOSEPH TYDINGS
EULOGY
June 6, 1968

Mr. President, Justice Holmes once said:
> As life is action and passion, it is required of a man that he should share the passion and action of his time, at peril of being judged not to have lived.

Robert Kennedy lived the action and passion of our time. He died in action. He spent his life; he gave his life in highest service to his country and to his fellow man. To those ignored he gave attention; to those in despair he gave hope; to those in need he gave help. To citizens blind to the fate of their fellow man he presented the discomforting specter of the other America. He gave himself.

Bob Kennedy, my friend, is dead. But the challenge of a newer world he pursued so selflessly remains. Let us be equal to that challenge.

In the long roll of history it will be marked for Bob Kennedy, as it was for his brother John: "There was a man." We will not soon forget these men or their compassion. As Pericles said centuries ago:
> Heroes have the whole earth for their tomb; and in lands far from their own—where the column with its epitaph declares it—there is enshrined in every breast a record unwritten with no tablet to preserve it, except that of the heart.

God have mercy upon the soul of Robert Kennedy. God have mercy upon his family. God have mercy upon us all.

REPRESENTATIVE EDITH GREEN
EULOGY
June 6, 1968

Mr. Speaker, we will all mourn the loss of something in the loss of Robert Kennedy. Some will mourn the loss of a leader; others, the loss of an innovator; still others, the loss of a Senator. Some will mourn the loss of a father and husband; others, the loss of a son, or a brother, or a friend. But I hope that we will not fail to mourn, quite simply, the loss of a man—a living, breathing, caring, and suffering man, a man who cannot live or breathe again, who will not have the supreme good fortune to care deeply about something in this country, or suffer from something ever again. A vibrant, joyful person is dead; his voice irrevocably stilled. I am certain that John Donne was right:

> Any man's death diminishes me, for I am involved in mankind;
> And therefore, never send to know for whom the bell tolls; It
> tolls for thee.

It was Goethe who said:

> "We ask not that a man be a hero, but only that he be everything
> that makes a man."

Robert Kennedy was such a man. And so I find myself admittedly a mourner. And a mourner must reminisce, however harsh the modern maxim: "Be thou not sentimental." And I discover that I am not reminiscing so much about the Senator, or the candidate, or the critic, or the leader of men, as I find myself reminiscing about the essential phenomenon which was the man himself. It was the man that strolled, barefoot and slumped in thought, down a gray, lonely beach in Oregon. It was the man who looked with a combination of confusion and compassion into the eyes of someone who has traveled many miles just to hate. It was the man who cheered his despondent supporters after defeat in Oregon. It was the man that could become impassioned about racketeering, critical and discouraged over our course in Vietnam, emotional about the disadvantaged in America, desperate about the inversion of our priorities at home and abroad—and he admitted it.

No amount of eulogy, no amount of regret or national soul-searching or academic analysis of the climate of our society, no amount of penitential legend-making, no pedestal in the hall of fame or grave site at Arlington will bring back the man to his family, his friends, and those who believed in him and his cause.

LETTER FROM PRINCE SIHANOUK TO
MRS. ROBERT KENNEDY

June 6, 1968

Madame Robert Kennedy
Washington, D.C.
U.S.A.

We have been stunned by the tragic death of Senator Robert Kennedy and we beg you, Madame, to accept for yourself and for your children our deep condolences and the assurance of our profound sympathy for the cruel tragedy befalling you. The Royal Government, the Cambodian people, and I myself wish to express our admiration and our respect to the Kennedy family whose sacrifices in the cause of peace, justice and liberty for the oppressed must not be in vain for the honor of the American people and the future of humanity. In homage to the memory of the deeply regretted deceased, Cambodia desires to free without condition the two American soldiers interned for a violation of our territory.

(signed)
Prince Norodom Sihanouk
Chief of State of Cambodia

STEVE BELL
PERSPECTIVE ABC RADIO NETWORK
June 9, 1968

My thoughts concern a man...not his politics. And these thoughts are motivated by that one question all my friends and acquaintances asked... from the moment I began covering the primaries and the Kennedy campaign for President. The question: "What is Bobby Kennedy really like?"

The answers you'll hear today are not from a personal friend of Senator Kennedy. But from one who's work gave him a special opportunity to observe Kennedy the public man and candidate. They are also answers that a correspondent would not normally put in a broadcast report...for fear of being labeled "unobjective." But now that the man is dead...I offer them for what they are.

My first impression of Robert Francis Kennedy was how small a man he was physically. He appeared much smaller than his brother, the late President. Robert Kennedy also appeared bland and almost detached from the people and events around him. It was the kind of first impression that made one think. He really is an ordinary type, trying to hitch a ride on his brother's memory.

But that first impression of Robert Kennedy changed. And it didn't take long for the transition to begin. And by the end of the Nebraska primary I was telling my friends, privately, that Robert Kennedy was the "most impressive" of the candidates. I still hadn't decided whom I would want to vote for in November...but Kennedy the campaigner was something special.

Maybe that transition began with the victory statement in Indianapolis. It really wasn't historic. But it was my own first impression of that easy Kennedy wit. A kind of spontaneous thing that doesn't come from people who are "detached." It comes instead from those who have a "feel" for other people. I don't even remember the quips...just the impression. At the time it didn't seem important enough to write down or save on tape.

There was also the way he spoke of a need for reconciliation among all the divisions in our society. Somehow the words had seemed out of place in this moment of political victory. They almost put a damper on the celebration.

It was in Nebraska, though, that my new image of Robert Kennedy began to take substance. And it was one shared by a number of us who covered the primaries together from morning till late at night...then talked and ate when we should have been sleeping. In Nebraska we suddenly began to realize that Robert Kennedy had a near obsession about the plight of the poor...especially the American Indian. That he was more than a politician when he talked over and over again about healing the divisions in America ...and helping the helpless to help themselves.

Don't get me wrong. Robert Kennedy was a political animal in every sense of the word. He had that "instinct" for the right move...the right thing to say...and the instinct for knowing where the political power really was in a given city or state...and how to make use of it.

But he always seemed to talk about things like the plight of the Indians when it wasn't the thing to do. And he kept hammering away at the plight of the poor and the non-whites...when there was more chance for political loss than gain.

For me, one of Kennedy's most impressive moments came at Creighton University in Omaha. In a question and answer session after the standard speech, one young man asked the candidate for his views on the draft. And Robert Kennedy explained again how he believed in a lottery system... and in doing away with student deferments.

The response included a number of boos...and very little applause. And with that, Kennedy was off and running. He gave a lecture on how student deferments left children of the affluent in school while children of the poor died on the battlefields. He said there was no problem for Robert Kennedy to get all ten of his children into some college somewhere in the U.S. despite their grade points, but other fathers with ten children weren't so fortunate.

Then came another question. A youth said, "But isn't the Army one way of getting young people out of the ghettos...and solving the ghetto problem?" At that, the man on the platform was no longer a candidate for anything. "I don't understand," he said, "how you can have that attitude at a Catholic University." "How can you sit on your duff and talk like that," he asked, "while black boys and poor whites from the South are dying in Vietnam?" If the war must be fought, then every young man has the same obligation.

Later that same day it began to rain as Senator Kennedy made a tour into Omaha's near north side—a black ghetto area that's seen more than its share of violence. But the crowds still lined the streets and many pounded on the raised top of the Kennedy convertible. Suddenly the motorcade stopped. Senator Kennedy had his dog Freckles put on the dry and comfortable press bus, the top of the convertible went down, and the candidate stood in the rain to shake hundreds of hands and talk with the drenched crowds. It was more than a campaign gesture, it was a lesson in reconciliation. And it included a short lecture on the need to end violence, and force needed change thru democratic processes.

That night was one of those I mentioned, where we sat at a table and shared our impressions of what we had seen and heard. Everyone was impressed—with Kennedy the man.

Another vivid impression came at Cleveland high school in Portland. Once again the off-the-cuff remarks of the candidate went to the plight of the American Indian. But now I understood. There was no politiking, only genuine feeling, as Robert Kennedy told that white, middle-class audience about the day he visited an Indian reservation—only to learn later that a baby died of starvation that same day, on that same reservation. Robert Kennedy said, "When that baby died, a little bit of me died too." And he meant it.

This was the truth about Robert Kennedy that I saw. He was a man with a cause. Committee work in the United States Senate had brought him face to face with the plight of the American Indian. He had attacked and analyzed the problem with the same determination and intensity that's become a stereotype of a Kennedy. And the problem had become a cause.

The pieces were falling into place. Now it was easy to see how this man, as a senate investigator and campaign manager for his brother, could be described as "ruthless." When he believed in a cause he meant to make things happen. When there were mistakes, they no doubt left bitter scars. It's the same kind of tenacity and total commitment that must have pulled the Kennedys from the Irish ghettos of Boston to wealth and unequaled position.

Ironically, it's my own impression that this sense of duty even propelled Robert Kennedy into a public life he didn't really relish. Several who knew him well have told me the candidate was a naturally shy man. And it was this shyness that I had mistaken for aloofness and detachment at that first meeting.

They say the suspected assassin hated Robert Kennedy partly because of the Kennedy wealth. But my own reaction from Indiana to California was just the opposite. I couldn't stop wondering at this rich man who drove himself and the rest of us with him to physical and mental exhaustion. How much easier it would have been to find fame, fortune, pleasure, or power in almost any other way. Or, to have been one of those jet-set dropouts from the anguish of those in this world who are in need.

In the final analysis, it was not a matter of agreeing with the policies he supported or even being willing to say, "Yes, this is the man I would have voted for to be President of the United States." Instead, it was a matter of seeing this man in a far different light than before. Few people have been so hated or so loved as political figures. That was a product of his intensity and commitment. But it often distorted the picture I came to see. And I keep wondering if it didn't play a roll in the mind of the assassin, too.

My last impression of Robert Kennedy was a kind of confirmation of what had gone before. And it came only a few minutes before I saw him lying there in that pool of blood...surrounded by a sea of terrified and agonized faces. In that final victory statement at the Ambassador Hotel in Los Angeles, Robert Kennedy did it again. He departed from the expected thank you's and the easy quips to talk about helping the helpless, healing the divisions in America, and ending the plague of violence. All that was missing was that quote from George Bernard Shaw, the one he used so often it had become a standing joke between the candidate and the reporters who followed him from one stop to the next.

The quote goes: "Some people see things as they are and ask why. I see things that never were, and ask why not." For me, that's what Robert Francis Kennedy was really like.

AMBASSADOR JAMES BELL
EULOGY
June 9, 1968

Senator Robert F. Kennedy was no stranger to this part of the world or to Malaysia. He had a vibrant interest in Asia and Asians. He was overwhelmingly involved with youth, and young countries like Malaysia, which he visited at the beginning of my assignment as Ambassador here. He burned with conviction about the importance of paying attention to what older men have called the younger generation, young leaders in the universities, in politics, in government, labor and all segments of society and in all nations, including our own. He was, himself, the embodiment of youth in constructive ferment. At thirty-five, he was appointed United States Attorney General, the youngest man to have held this office since 1814. He was a symbol of change, an architect of reform, a totally fearless champion of social justice.

He forced his country's eyes to the truth and held them there, to the nation's glory and its shame. Glory for our achievements and for the further greatness lying within the reach of the American people—shame for the tasks yet to be accomplished to fulfill the dreams of Jefferson and Lincoln.

Above all, he had courage, what in slang Americans call "guts." The guts to see evil and injustice in naked terms and to lead men, even to drive them, to eradicate these. As Attorney General, he broke the defiance of Alabama in opening the doors of its State University to those of all races, even though to do so took the employment of the United States Army.

The civil rights movement in the United States—indeed, the fight for social justice throughout the world—owes much of its achievement to the driving fervor which Robert Kennedy brought to the fore, both during the Kennedy Administration, in the United States Senate and in the campaign for the 1968 Democratic presidential nomination in which he was engaged at the time of his tragic death.

We honor here today a man who was proud to be an American and of whom all Americans can be proud. I think that Robert Kennedy knew clearly, more than most of us, that those who are willing to fight for their convictions take on great risk. But I think that he knew, too, and took satisfaction in the knowledge, that crusades do not die with the crusader. I know that I personally am the richer in spirit and wiser in my vision for having known and, on occasion, had the privilege of working with Robert F. Kennedy. The world is a better place for his brief but burning transit of this life. The improvement will continue. This is what he would most want.

W. F. MINOR
THE NEW ORLEANS TIMES-PICAYUNE
June 9, 1968

Mississippi had been a hostile land for Robert F. Kennedy much of the time he was on the public scene, but he came—three times in all—to meet and touch its pople and to stand amid some of its direst social ills.

In the history of Mississippi, the name of Robert Kennedy must be etched from an event in 1962 which brought Mississippi into the greatest confrontation with the federal power since the Civil War.

His role in the episode as the man who directed the federal side in putting Negro James Meredith into the University of Mississippi is what had engendered most the antipathy for the bushy-haired, ruddy New Englander among Mississippi whites.

But Kennedy lived long enough to win over many who thought him the sole devil in the Meredith affair, and he came in later days to provide hope and sustenance to the poor and hungry of the state.

In the heat of the crisis over Meredith, Mississippians had viewed defiant Governor Ross Barnett as the hero of the day and Attorney General Robert Kennedy as his ruthless antagonist in Washington.

The defiance of Barnett to the federal government ended in a bloody stand by thousands of Mississippians on the campus of the university the night of September 30, 1962. Five hundred federal marshals were set upon by a screaming mob as gunshots rang out in the night and broken bricks and bottles came hurtling at the federal officers out of the darkness. To save the marshals and put Meredith into the university, army troops were moved to the campus.

Later the behind-the-scenes story of Barnett talking with Attorney General Kennedy during the height of the Mississippi tension, offering to make a deal on the Meredith showdown, began to unfold from various printed sources.

Eventually, in March 1966, Robert Kennedy came in person to Mississippi, to the campus of Ole Miss and related with remarkable detail what had taken place between himself and Barnett in the Meredith crisis negotiations.

That day in the university coliseum, more than 5000 Ole Miss students—the young people from the state's smallest and largest towns—stood and in a tremendous outburst of applause and cheers acquitted Robert Kennedy of the Mississippi charge he had been the culprit in the Meredith affair.

To this reporter who has witnessed receptions given Mississippi political figures over two decades, the response to Kennedy that day at Ole Miss contained more spontaneity and unrestrained enthusiasm than any state politician has ever received.

Kennedy and his wife Ethel stood apprehensively in the doorway of their plane that day when it arrived in Oxford. The famed Kennedy smile was not evident. But when the friendly crowd of students waiting outside surged forward, the Kennedy smile flashed and he surged into a sea of hands.

Few know that during the tragic night of September 30, 1962, Robert Kennedy could have given the order which probably would have caused the deaths of many Mississippians, but he never gave it.

Repeatedly, the beleaguered marshals and the cadre of Justice Department men at the Lyceum Building asked for permission to open fire on the attacking mob.

In their ranks were some of the best marksmen in the United States, border patrolmen, and federal prison guards. Their ranks had been bloodied throughout the wild evening, and sixty of them lay wounded.

But at the other end of the command-post telephone, Robert Kennedy withheld the order to open fire and during the entire night, although the marshals were under attack constantly for nearly six hours, he would not give permission to fire upon the attackers.

Kennedy returned to Mississippi in April 1967 in still a different role—as a United States Senator who wanted to know about the poverty conditions in the state.

It was to be nothing more than a formal hearing about poverty, as congressional committees are accustomed to holding. But what Kennedy heard in that hearing compelled him to look farther into the heart and soul of poverty and hunger which was talked about.

So this wealthy, patrician son of New England, on a warm Southern day, went off into the very bowels of stark poverty in the Negro shacks of the Mississippi Delta Country. In one stench-ridden house after another Kennedy plunged right inside the tiny hovels and looked and talked with the occupants.

To anyone who felt until that moment he understood something about what poverty and deprivation meant, there was a revelation which can only come from the oozing smell of poverty which emerges from the tiny kitchen or bedroom in a Delta shack.

For just a moment, this writer and Senator Kennedy stood alone in a dank little kitchen where a wood stove seemed remarkably uncooked on, and a pitiful snatch of beans and rice and a few cans were in evidence to feed a family of eight.

"Have you ever seen anything like this before?" this reporter asked.

Kennedy didn't hesitate. "Yes, I have. I've seen it in Southeast Asia and in Harlem."

Bone-weary after a day full of going from house to house over a broad sweep of the Delta, patting Negro children with distended stomachs and holding his ear close for elderly Negroes to tell him of their situations, he took off for Washington. But he did not forget those poor and hungry. He kept their fight going in Congress.

Many said in Mississippi that the conditions which Kennedy observed and talked about were distortions. Just a month ago, a doctor from the Delta, a county health official, came here to speak to the Mississippi Medical Association. In effect, he confirmed what Robert Kennedy has seen for himself in this state.

MARTIN ARNOLD
THE NEW YORK TIMES
June 7, 1968

He had come to New York, like so many others, to make a career, although, of course, it was different because he was Robert F. Kennedy and the career might reach to the White House.

Sometimes greeted bitterly as a carpetbagger, or with wry jokes about his need for a guidebook, he would respond that people did not understand that the nasal twang in his voice was a "Bronx accent" (as a youngster he had lived in Riverdale and Bronxville, N.Y.) or a "Glen Cove accent" (when he decided to run for the Senate, he rented a house in Glen Cove, L.I.)

Once, a short time after he was elected to the Senate, he made a luncheon date to meet his sister-in-law, Mrs. John F. Kennedy, at a French restaurant. His staff, knowing less about the city than he did, led him to La Bonwit, a diner on Fortieth Street between Seventh and Eighth Avenues, where the customers were in shirt sleeves and the manager, wearing a T shirt, started wiping the table tops when he saw the famous man. Mrs. Kennedy was waiting at La Grenouille.

To the end, despite his light references to having come from out-of-state, some people in New York still deeply resented him as "that carpetbagger." Many, however, accepted him and, indeed, seemed proud to have such a famous Senator.

When Senator Kennedy settled in the city shortly after his election in 1964, he did it in a way that every New Yorker or out-of-towner would like to: He took an apartment in the large, glamorous United Nations Plaza overlooking the East River.

And he enjoyed the city: the theater and the parties he went to on nearly every night that he was free; the professional football games at Yankee Stadium; and La Caravelle, "21," Lafayette, and other restaurants.

One rainy night, driving uptown after attending an off-Broadway production, the Senator's car stopped at an intersection. A drunk was sprawled across the sidewalk, his head over the curb. Several people stepped over the man and cars drove past. Senator Kennedy stopped his car, and all the men in it got out and helped the drunk to his feet.

A long discussion as to whether a policeman should be called followed, and it was finally decided not to call one because the drunk might get in trouble. "You see what *my* city is like, Jim? You don't have things like that at home," the Senator said to James Whittaker, a friend from Seattle. The drunk was sent on his way.

Because of the carpetbagger issue, and because he believed that all things connected with a Kennedy should be first, Robert F. Kennedy brought his natural competitiveness to his being a New Yorker. He made countless tours of the state, urging mayors and other local officials to take advantage of federally aided programs.

"New Yorkers are paying most of the taxes, but other small cities in other states are taking advantage of the federal programs," he would say in meetings in city halls. in school auditoriums and at club meetings. "We are giving the money and they are spending it."

Sometimes, despite the squealing and cheering of local people, the trips merely added to the list of those who did not like him. One such person was a local school superintendent whom Senator Kennedy would caustically chide as incompetent. And Senator Kennedy would remember, too. "How would you like your children to be educated by that fellow?" he would ask an aide a year later, recalling the superintendent by name and city.

There were places in the state that had special meaning to him. Glens Falls was one. The old Fulton Fish Market was another. He considered Bedford-Stuyvesant and Harlem his special constituencies. And Bedford-Stuyvesant and Harlem considered him their special Senator.

Senator Kennedy had begun his Senate campaign early in the morning among heaps of shimmering mackerel at the Fulton Fish Market, and he promised to revisit the market, win or lose, after Election Day.

Early in the morning on Nov. 5, 1964, he left a victory celebration of family and friends at Delmonico's to go to the market, where he was recalled by fishmongers with glad cries. They gave him a halibut to hold, and he did.

One balmy night in September while he was campaigning for the Senate, he arrived several hours late in Glens Falls, and was, surprisingly, greeted by 4000 people, many in pajamas, who were waiting to cheer him.

So Glens Falls became a special city for him, and after greeting the fishmongers, he went to the Carlyle Hotel for three hours' sleep and then flew with his wife, Ethel, to that upstate city to thank the citizens for helping to elect him. Again he drew a crowd of nearly 4000.

He spoke very often of Bedford-Stuyvesant and Harlem, and in the Brooklyn Negro slum he set up two corporations to bring in private industry and to link that industry with neighborhood self-help programs.

As a political leader in the state he was open to criticism. He tended to work outside the regular Democratic party organization, setting up instead his own parallel organization of bright young men, and most Democratic political leaders resented this, particularly since one of the rationales of his coming into the state was to modernize the party.

One Democratic state leader put it this way in an interview: "They [the leaders] hate him because they are afraid of him. I doubt many of them would cross him, but he's unsure of his power with the leaders. He'd rather go to the voters."

Senator Kennedy particularly liked the upstate areas, the small towns, where he was greeted by flag-waving and by hundreds of children. His legislative record reflected this.

His amendments, the ones bearing his name, deal primarily with state problems. The Appalachia amendment, passed over the objection of Governor Rockefeller, brought $27-million in federal aid to the southwestern part of the state. Another amendment, cosponsored by his Republican colleague, Senator Jacob K. Javits, allowed 100,000 Spanish-speaking Puerto Ricans to vote. A third Kennedy amendment, passed in 1965, authorized the Federal Government to establish a universal system to test student progress in schools receiving federal aid.

He also enjoyed walking in New York City because, he said often, "everybody's always in such a hurry to get home they don't see me."

In May last year the Senator, his wife, and nine of their children took the kind of trip that had become associated with his name. They spent two days bouncing through the rapids of the upper Hudson River.

After Mr. Kennedy tumbled out of his one-man kayak and was swept about half a mile past jagged boulders in the turbulent water, he pulled himself, dripping and shivering, up the river bank. Ever mindful of the carpetbagger charges, he asked a reporter: "What are you going to say now? That I was the first Senator who ever fell in the Hudson River?"

BRUCE BIOSSAT
NEWSPAPER ENTERPRISE ASSOCIATION
June 5, 1968

Robert F. Kennedy, the fourth of his family to be struck by tragedy, has moved across the American political scene for a decade in the very eye of a storm of controversy.

Some elements that make him a storm center can be fathomed and some cannot. He is loved and admired, hated and feared more passionately perhaps than has been true of any man in this country's public life in modern times—even Franklin D. Roosevelt.

Professional poll-takers who sketch out candidate profiles long ago learned that this churning, driving man of forty-two, with his craggy face and unruly shock of hair is seen by Americans as a puzzling mosaic of contrasting impressions.

The catalogue of negatives is astonishing—"ruthless, too ambitious, erratic, unreliable, too emotional, trading on his late brother's name, using his family's wealth to win high office, questing after public adulation."

Yet countless Americans see him as warm, friendly, aggressive in pursuit of useful political and national goals, a fitting successor to his martyred brother, John Kennedy.

Robert Kennedy himself unquestionably has been stunned this spring at the depth and breadth of the animosity he seems to stir in so many quarters. On a campaign airplane he said to me as he has to others:

"I'm the only candidate who has ever managed to unite business, labor, the organization Democrats and the intellectuals. They're all against me."

A few days later, a key figure in the California political world offered this in partial explanation of the sturdy opposition to Kennedy within the leading elements of his own party:

"Politicians do not like men who are tougher than they are, and Bob Kennedy is tougher than they."

When he campaigned for the U. S. Senate in New York four years ago, I asked him how he reacted to the then already familiar charge of ruthlessness. He thought a long while before answering : "I think that is what happens to you when you try to do things."

That comment may be close to the core of it. Reporters traveling with him on the 1968 primary trail have been struck by the fact that the fear of him persists among many Americans even as he talks more conservatively than his rival, Senator Eugene McCarthy, but yet talks of doing things to alter the nation's course in war and in its troubled cities.

One perceptive observer feels that this image of the driving activist is enough alone to alarm many Americans who may see the need for some change but do not want too much of it. Says this man: "Looking at the other candidates, in both parties, these people do not think their election as president would affect the course of events too drastically. But they are pretty sure that if Bob Kennedy were in the White House their world would be different—in ways they can hardly guess."

An old friend and former close associate of Kennedy's recently told me flatly that he believes the label of "ruthless" was indeed applicable to some of the Senator's behavior. Yet he feels that in some ways this charge, made too sweepingly and repeated too often by people who have had no experience with such behavior from him, works in his favor as he campaigns the nation.

"When they see him in person," says this friend, "many people decide that he isn't all that ruthless."

A good many reporters evidently have been thus affected. Some who have joined his traveling troupe with a certain built-in hostility toward Kennedy have been transformed into stout admirers after a week or two of close contact.

At intimate range, many find him very warm, considerate of their needs, witty, tough but often quite generous in his judgments of others in public life, genuinely fond of people.

In California not long ago, he quietly told some reporters he would be happy to have them bring their wives along on the press plane to ease the hardship of long separation. Several times, he confided to newsmen that he is deeply fond of the young idealists who have flocked to McCarthy's banner and hopes to win some of them to his side if his own candidacy flourishes.

Observers who have never watched him campaign in person are always amazed by the easy, quick rapport he develops with a crowd. His bantering exchanges are so continuous that sometimes his appearances have the air of an audience-participation show on television.

To a huge, noisy, racially mixed throng in an auditorium at Camden, N. J., he shouted:

"How many of you ever heard of Charles Croft? [long pause] None of you, none of you! Well, he was the Earl of Camden for whom this city was named."

Usually the lighthearted chatter evokes laughter and warm response. It even works on frosty audiences like the City Club in Portland, Ore., where business and professional leaders found themselves laughing in spite of themselves. They broke up when he said: "Somebody just took a poll of 500 businessmen and I got one vote . . . I understand they're looking for him."

Though Kennedy can be sharp and short-tempered, he often deals with hecklers and hostile signs in crowds with great tolerance and wit.

In Omaha a bull-voiced man shouting at him finally forced the Senator to halt his speech. He turned to look at his wife, Ethel, and said with a smile: "Ethel, I'm very sorry to have to tell you this, but I'm afraid the vote in

Omaha is not going to be unanimous."

All this good-spirited campaigning makes its inevitably strong impression upon thousands and thousands of Americans who feel the touch of his charismatic presence. Those who pore over election statistics find a definite link between his personal travel routes and healthy votes for him in primary tests.

Nevertheless, it does not wipe out the negative impressions which cling tenaciously to him. With some people, including some prominent figures in his chosen party, the distaste for Kennedy seems so great that he cannot win no matter what he does.

A few years ago he met privately in New York with some strong-minded Negro leaders, including Professor Kenneth Clark and author James Baldwin. Reports later filtered out that he had shown an appalling ignorance of the Negro's plight and seemed unable to communicate effectively.

Today, his string of primary victories in such states as California, Nebraska, Indiana, as well as the District of Columbia has demonstrated he has an 80 to 90 percent hold on the nation's troubled Negro citizenry.

The earlier criticism has died, only to be replaced with new charges that he is "too close" to the Negroes in the turbulent racial struggle. Even McCarthy has made special note of Kennedy's identification with "bloc votes," a clear reference to his immense Negro support.

Similarly, Kennedy was often chided in earlier years for playing hero to young Americans. When McCarthy entered the presidential race, some of these young people flocked to him and launched what came to be known, admiringly, as the "children's crusade." Almost lost from sight was the fact, too, that when primary votes were counted, Kennedy actually was winning the support of people under thirty by margins up to two to one over McCarthy.

Twists of this sort suggested that, whatever his political future, he was never likely to escape being the storm center he has been for so long. It is the country's tragedy as well as his that he became a would-be assassin's target as he continued to move in the hurricane's eye of controversy.

LOUDON WAINWRIGHT
LIFE
May 17, 1968

When it was all over in Indiana, Robert Kennedy, surrounded by staff workers and friends, stood in front of a television set and watched himself in a victory interview. It had been given just a little earlier in the evening, and Kennedy studied the picture with a deep intentness, as if he weren't quite sure what his voice was going to say or what the next expression might reveal. At one point the crowd around him laughed at his dry answer to a question, but Kennedy's lip merely bent in the slightest show of amusement and then the face was straight again. In an age of images, he seemed to be testing his own for flaws, and if he did not look satisfied, he surely could take some small pleasure from the figures that indicated that somebody out there liked him. In fact, if the mildest sort of inference may be drawn from the Indiana primary, it is that the "Hate Bobby" people seem to be in some sort of trouble.

Of course, it's a long time until August and longer to November, and the list of offenses any good hater can repeat is widely available. The old Joe McCarthy association won't go away, nor will that awful amount of money, nor will the name, whose magic for Bobby is allegedly black. New real or imagined reasons for hate may arise, and they could hurt. But the fact remains that Robert Kennedy won in Indiana, and he did it because he was willing to expose himself to great numbers of people and was able to convince a substantial proportion of them that perhaps he wasn't such a bad man after all. Though a hater might scoff, it is even likely that he conveyed the impression that his concerns were genuine and deep and that he meant what he said.

Getting used to the possibility that Kennedy cares might prove too great a task for a skeptical electorate, but one can be very sure that this candidate will devote an enormous effort to demonstrating that he does indeed. This drive was visible in Indiana in many forms. His repeated latenesses at stops along the campaign journey were often the result of totally unexpected pauses at a house or a face or a group of children who had gone to sleep on the roof of a car while they waited for him. Election hokum, some might say, overripe fruits for the hungry cameras, but it is certain that his exhausting sallies had a profound effect on the people visited, just as his aching hand moved those thousands it reached for in passing. Hysteria, maybe, but the truth is that when he put out his hand, they lunged for the uncommon touch.

At other times, his concern was much less loving. Before an audience at a medical school in Indianapolis, Kennedy's hand trembled as he took a drink of water. The quality of dislike for him in the well-scrubbed, intelligent crowd was obvious, and he was plainly nervous. When he had finished his speech about possible programs for medical care, the applause was decidedly not deafening, and the questions which came immediately were pointed and aggressive. Suddenly the candidate himself turned aggressive. To the shouted question: "Who's going to pay for all this?" Kennedy called back sharply, "You are!" and then proceeded to deliver himself of a lecture in which he virtually accused the students of not living up to their community responsibilities, of being involved only in their own selfish interests.

He chopped on, perilously close to the breaking moment when they might boo him right out the hall. At one point he even wondered aloud why there were not more black faces in the crowd and then described the problems of educating impoverished, undernourished children who were "too weak to work, too ill to listen." When he finished by talking about the need for people to make a "great effort to try to understand one another, to reach each other across barriers that exist," the clapping was solid and dotted with cheers. And surely some of those who hated Bobby hated him more then because of the nasty glimpse he had given them of the smug state of their own consciences.

On the last night of the Indiana campaign the candidate sat late and talked. He had clearly been stimulated by the pace of the campaign and he spoke with special enthusiasm of the people he had seen in the small towns. There, he felt, many of the men and women he had spoken to had listened and actually wondered what they might do about some of the problems he raised. His mind skipped on, and he spoke about a comparative study that had been done on the differences in drawings made by white and black children. When poor Negro children drew pictures of houses, he recalled, they seldom drew a sun over them. "Have you ever noticed," he asked, "that the faces of poor kids are much more alert and bright than the faces of kids who are more comfortable?" He had, and he had also noticed that at the age of thirteen or fourteen the faces changed, as if all curiosity and expectation had gone. A candidate who remarks on such matters is going to get harder to hate.

JOSEPH ALSOP
WASHINGTON POST SYNDICATE

The youthful figure strides down into the crowded auditorium with the same oddly decisive swiftness of movement that marked his brother's public appearances. You find yourself thinking, both sadly and nostalgically, of that other hard race through the primaries that now seems to belong to another age, yet was only eight years ago.

The big crowd has been waiting over an hour without serious impatience—for the welcome is very warm. At a signal, the countless young people in the crowd begin singing the campaign song, which is a revised version of Woody Guthrie's "This Land Is Your Land."

> This man [they sing] is your man
> This man is my man,
> From California to the New York Island,
> From the Redwood forests to the Gulf Stream waters.

They seem to mean every word of it, and despite the pseudo-poetry, it is somehow rather stirring. Then there are the usual introductions; and finally the candidate moves to the microphone, looking strangely young despite the deep lines that have invaded his face, with the famous lock of hair, now grown longer again, hanging lankly down over his forehead.

He begins lightly, with small jokes; and he has an even greater knack of wry humor than his brother had. Then, when the last laugh dies away, a note of seriousness and urgency invades his somewhat harsh but pleasant voice; and he begins his recitation of America's all too numerous problems.

"I say that's not acceptable; that's not satisfactory!" So he dismisses each successive problem, hitting his right hand, hard, down into his left hand's palm for extra emphasis. Sometimes he adds, with malice, "That's not the politics of joy and happiness." And at the end, he gets a big hand when he sums: "If I'm elected President of the United States, I intend to do something about *all* these matters!"

For the political handicappers, the performance is strikingly interesting. The style is neither elegant nor polished; the statements are made staccato and there are frequent repetitions; yet what comes through most strongly is a sense of deep and true concern, a feeling that this man genuinely cares very greatly about "these matters." And it is just this that makes Robert F. Kennedy a mighty effective campaigner.

For the political analyst, too, what is said is strikingly interesting. You keep wondering, in truth, why so many conservative persons suppose that this man wears radical horns and a New Left tail. That was certainly the impression he managed to convey in the frenetic speeches before President Johnson's renunciation; but there is nothing of that in what he says now.

Even on Vietnam, he merely calls for "An Honorable Peace," with emphasis on the word "honorable"; and he adds realistically, "maybe we can't get an honorable peace, but I'm glad we're trying." And in what he has to say about the race problems and riots, about economics and government, about poverty and its remedies, there is nothing that ought to alarm or disturb any reasonable man or woman.

Such was Bobby Kennedy when he was covering South Dakota's small towns in a whirlwind tour a few days ago. Such he had been before, and was again on the stump in Nebraska. Such he will be, no doubt, in Oregon and California. Watching him in action in this manner, it must be added, you are endlessly puzzled at the strange disparity between the man and the "image" of himself that he has somehow managed to project.

He is supposed to be a ruthless and calculating politician, as well as a near-sympathizer of the New Left. He is in fact a romantic politician, far too given to taking dares, and much too willing to listen to the siren songs that warmly responsive audiences always sing.

These latter characteristics led him perilously close, in the last two years, to accepting the role of Hero of a minority cult—which is always fatal in American politics. One can even date the beginning of the process, in the sunlight of a glorious day, with a splendidly young and hopeful audience, in the Greek theater at Berkeley two years ago. And because he went so far toward becoming a cult hero, he must now make extra efforts to appeal to the American center.

That is one side of the problem. The other is the supposed ruthlessness and calculation. The truth is that if he had been truly ruthless and calculating, he would be in an immeasurably stronger position at this moment. He was instead hot-blooded, combative, and compassionate. He still is; and this is a political combination that is often dangerous to the politician himself.

If you know this man at all well, you can have no doubt about his large-heartedness, his depth of feeling, his attachment to America. You can have no doubt, either, about his remarkable equipment to deal with all the grim internal problems that now face America. The trouble is, however, that there may be too few who know him at all well.

ART BUCHWALD
THE WASHINGTON POST SYNDICATE
July 11, 1968

I went down the rapids of the Colorado River in the Grand Canyon with Senator Robert Kennedy and his family and friends last week. There were forty-two people in the party, including singer Andy Williams, mountain climber Jim Whittaker, pro football player George Plimpton, skier Willy Schaeffler, publisher Otis Chandler, and thirty-five Kennedy children.

I was the only one in condition to make the trip, but in spite of this my father didn't want me to go. "It's all right for Kennedy to go down the rapids because he can walk on the water, but you're going to have to swim."

I assured him that the Kennedys would never do anything dangerous, but it was hard to persuade him. He said, "It's as safe to go down the Colorado River with Bobby Kennedy in a raft as it is to sail up the Nile with General Moshe Dayan."

Despite my father's fears I'm glad I went. You really don't get to know a man until you've taken a rapid with him. The trouble is, Bobby Kennedy took a lot of rapids, and he took them on an air mattress. Ethel, mother of ten, also took the rapids *out* of the raft, and of course her children took the rapids out of the raft, so there was nothing left for the rest of the party to do but leave the raft as well.

The best way to take a rapid is to float feet first on your life preserver, just in case you hit a rock. But I invented a new way of doing it. If you keep your mouth open you can swallow most of the water you're going over, which makes it half as rough. My wife had to give me mouth-to-mouth resuscitation every night when we camped, but no one noticed it because everyone thought we were just kissing under the stars.

If you're ever going down the rapids with the Kennedys, it's best to choose a river that isn't surrounded by cliffs. Every morning after breakfast Bobby would look up at another mountain and ask Mount Everest climber Jim Whittaker, "Do you think it's tough to climb?" If Whittaker said no, Bobby would look at another mountain. "What about that one?" If Whittaker said, "It's impossible," Bobby would call the party together and say, "that's the one we're going up," and pretty soon Ethel, mother of ten, the Kennedy children and the rest of the group would be scrambling up the mountain in 110-degree heat.

After the mountain had been conquered, everyone would return to the rafts to take some more rapids. By the third day I was starting to have a great deal of respect for my father, and I wouldn't take off my life preserver even to get into my sleeping bag.

Probably the most dangerous part of the trip was the last day, when we arrived at a place laughingly called Phantom Lodge, seven miles down, at the bottom of the Grand Canyon. The only ways to get out of the canyon were to walk out in 119-degree heat, ride a burro out along the same trail, or pretend you're going to die so they'll send a helicopter for you. I had rehearsed the death scene for three days, and by the time we arrived at Phantom Lodge I was barely breathing.

Bobby opted to climb up the seven miles, as did the Kennedy children, and when Ethel, mother of ten, said she would climb out too, the rest of the party were too embarrassed to say they'd rather go by helicopter.

Fearful that they would cancel the helicopter, I stopped breathing when Bobby and Jim Whittaker came up to me to see if they could persuade me to change my mind.

Bobby said, "Why don't you want to climb the mountain?"

I just smiled weakly and replied, "Because it's there."

GEORGE SULLIVAN
THE BOSTON HERALD TRAVELER
June 6, 1968

Harvard Stadium was never as silent as it was yesterday morning.

I know because that is where I went to meditate after receiving news of a tragedy that had occurred nearly 3000 miles away. People retreated to many places to pray and try to comprehend that catastrophe. They went to churches and dark rooms and other places of solitude to be alone and try to cope with this twisted and awful thing.

I went to an empty football field, a seemingly odd place to mourn the fate of a United States Senator and presidential candidate fighting for his life. But for me it was not a strange place at all, for it was in Harvard Stadium that I first knew that man and formed a friendship which I have treasured for nearly twenty-two of my thirty-four years. I have known the man as an Attorney General of the United States and as a Senator from New York. But in many ways I prize more the memories of the earlier years, for they are basic to the knowledge of the man who was the rise to such rare and enormous offices.

So let me tell you what kind of an athlete Bob Kennedy was—and what kind of a sports enthusiast he has always been—because the telling of it reveals an insight into the type of man he is.

You must understand from the start that my story is basically unflavored by what happened in Los Angeles yesterday. It is written objectively—although with the heaviest of hearts—and without glorification. Such is not needed, because it is compiled from simple facts which speak eloquently enough for themselves and need no embellishment. And so it is the same story I would have told you the day, month, or year before yesterday if you had asked me.

Let me also make clear from the beginning that while I am a friend of Bob, I am not an intimate one. But that only makes what I want to tell you all the more significant. That I've been a comparative nobody over the span of this friendship—first as a kid, later as a sports writer—only accentuates the portrait.

I have known the man since I was twelve. That was in 1946 when I was a water boy for the Harvard football team on which Robert F. Kennedy '48 was a junior and reserve end.

Dick Harlow's 1946 and 1947 Crimson editions were not typical collegiate football teams as we know them today. World War II had just ended and the team was composed mostly of service veterans just back from overseas. The medium age was twenty-three to twenty-four and I believe one of them—Johnny Gorczinski—was approaching thirty. And they had a unique maturity a youngster could admire.

The 1946 team sort of adopted me and another water boy, Ted Rattigan, off the field as well as on. We both lived in Cambridge's modest Kerry Corner section within the shadow of Harvard.

On weekends we were the guests of the players at the Harvard Varsity Club. Many of the athletes resided there, and others who roomed instead in the "house" dormitories still used the club as their base of operation.

The athletes taught a couple of twelve year olds how to play pool on those weekends. They also taught us something about politics, too—the favorite topic of conversation outside of football shop talk. An ex-sailor named Kennedy and a former navigator-bombardier named Ken O'Donnell were always discussing and arguing politics and their teammates eagerly joined in.

These were full weekends for a couple of youngsters, and activities were not confined to the Varsity Club. The players often took their two "mascots" around town on their errands and to events like Celtics games. The principle modes of transportation—shared by the players—were a somewhat beat-up black convertible belonging to Kennedy and a war surplus Jeep owned by a student manager. Both invited pneumonia—the convertible's heater always seemed out of order, and the Jeep's canvas top was shredded and did absolutely nothing to keep out snow and rain.

The next season—1947—was much more of the same. There was one change, among others, however. Kennedy—at 5' 10", 165—won a starting berth for the season's opener.

In all frankness, despite his enormous popularity among most of his teammates, Bob's promotion wasn't greeted with total joy. A few suggested the Kennedy name had contributed to his choice as a starter. It was a bum rap. Ask anyone who knew how Harlow evaluated football talent. He was a coach influenced by only one thing, and that wasn't anyone's name.

Harvard scored a 52–0 victory over Western Maryland in the opener, and six of those points came on a six yard O'Donnell-to-Kennedy pass. It proved to be Bob's first and last touchdown for the Crimson.

Despite pinching a neck nerve in that game, Bob had a special collar fitted and practiced the next week. At least he did for a day or two. During a scrimmage he tried to block an opposing back near the sideline—and missed, crashing heavily into an equipment wagon out of bounds. But he scrambled to his feet and returned to his position. Three days later he collapsed. X rays revealed he'd been practicing on a broken leg.

So Bob's Harvard football career was ended, although he wore No. 86 twice again as he made token appearances against Brown and Yale at season's end.

It is probably presumptuous and unfair to suggest who Bob's closest friends were at Harvard—the guys who were always needling his non-smoking, non-drinking and clean-living habits. That's impossible to gauge. But I don't think any of them will complain if I top the list with Ken and Cleo O'Donnell, Nick Rodis, Chuck Glynn, Bill Brady, and Chuck Roche. They were among the ushers in the wedding party when Bob and Ethel were married in June, 1950.

I talked with one by telephone: Rodis, now athletic director at Brandeis. Besides the need to commiserate, I suppose, I wanted to double check on my assessment on Bob's abilities at Harvard. I didn't want to risk possible miscalculation since I had observed them as a youngster and decided to get the impressions of one of his contemporaries. And the views of Rodis—who headed the State Department's athletic programs for five years until joining Brandeis last summer and who currently along with Stan Musial co-chairs the Sportsmen for Kennedy Committee—coincided precisely with mine.

These are Nick's words:

> "Harlow said it all for Bob's football ability when he once told me after practice one day that Bobby was the toughest kid pound for pound—more guts and zip—he had coached since Bobby Green 10 years before. Bob was a tiger and without question earned the starter's job. Because of limited size, he wasn't devastating on offense, although not bad either. But on defense he was outstanding—almost impossible to knock off his feet and tough as nails. So while we might have had better pass-catchers in '47, Bob still deserved the starter's job because he put the entire game together—defense and offense—in that day of one platoon football.
>
> "And he did it with heart.
>
> "That heart is also his key as a person and always has been since the day I first bumped into him in his sailor suit in 1946. That bull peddled by some in recent years—the part about him supposedly being cold and ruthless—has always infuriated me. Nothing could be further from the truth. He was a man with a golden heart if there ever was one.
>
> "All the fellows on the team at Harvard knew he was extremely wealthy. But nobody tried to take advantage of him. Yet anyone in trouble always knew he could go to Bobby—and would. He was always the first guy wanting to help and be with you when the chips were down.
>
> "And he has never changed over the years. Never. He is the most considerate man I've ever known. And don't take my word for it. Ask anyone who has ever worked alongside of him—on the football field or anywhere else."

I can vouch for that with many examples, but will restrict myself to one.

My employment as water boy had lasted only one year. In the summer of 1947 an ankle-to-thigh cast was placed on my left leg—to remain there for the better part of two years. So, I could no longer be employed at $1 a day to carry the water buckets and help tote the equipment. Out of sympathy, I guess, my pal Teddy resigned too. From then on we were strictly "mascots" —and settled for those wonderful weekends and being privvy to the team's secret practice sessions (developing into shutter bugs, becoming the team's "official snapshot photographers" as the players used to say).

Our only problem was on game days. We always joined the players as they headed from Dillon Field House across the lawn to the stadium for pre-game warm-ups. They'd embrace us among their ranks and march us through the players' entrance into the field.

The problem was, you had to show a ticket to get within the enclosed outer perimeter of Soldiers Field in those days as well as once again to get inside the stadium itself. We couldn't afford those tickets. So every game morning pal Teddy would boost me to the top of the ten-foot, spike-topped fence along Soldiers Field and I'd jump—cast and all. We'd often get caught inside before we'd reach the field house and would be ejected—only to repeat the process a second and sometimes third time. But we never missed our "appointment."

The players never knew about these acrobatics—they assumed we had passes, and I guess we were too proud to enlighten them. Bob was the first to find out about it and roasted me for risking breaking my neck. From then on, Bob—his own left leg encased in a smaller cast—insisted on picking us up at my home in his convertible on future game mornings and driving us to the field house. And he did—often driving out to the suburbs after collecting us to pick up his date on route to the stadium.

I've often thought since that those girls must have been delighted to find two thirteen-year-old boys along on their dates.

And I've never failed to remind Bob in later years that he was an excellent chauffeur. After all, how many people can claim they had a future Attorney General, brother and adviser of a President, Senator and presidential candidate chauffeuring him around?

This is only one example, but I could cite others over the years. And these were the things—among so much—that scrambled through my mind yesterday as I stood in the empty stadium.

The sun high above seemed a mockery. It was shining brilliantly.

JULES WITCOVER
NEWHOUSE NEWSPAPERS
May 29, 1968

Senator Robert F. Kennedy, the first of his family to suffer an election defeat after twenty-seven straight winning efforts, sat in his shirtsleeves in his Benson Hotel Suite, tie off but still wearing the PT 109 tieclasp that had been the symbol of Kennedy political invincibility. He had a heavily watered-down drink in his hand, and he was in a quiet, reflective mood—not bitter, not shocked, not even transparently disappointed, just resigned.

Well-wishers and aides in the suite moved deferentially toward him, spoke a few words of encouragement, then moved on, not wishing to intrude excessively on this awkward time.

Once he moved into the bedroom, where aides like Ted Sorensen, Dick Goodwin, Pierre Salinger, Fred Dutton, plus other newer team members who had not tasted the sweetest Kennedy victories of earlier years, held their post-mortem. Then he came out again, smiling, quietly cordial, fielding questions with patience. His wife, Ethel, as unassuming as ever, talked with friends and acted for all the world that losing was routine for a Kennedy, which of course it was not.

Kennedy, sitting on the arm of a chair, said he knew a week ago that he was in trouble when he failed to get a responsive reaction from factory workers in the Portland area. He could tell, he said, they weren't tuned in, that he wasn't communicating to them.

He asked aides where he had run well and where poorly, and took the information as much like the campaign manager he once was—matter-of-factly—as like the candidate he now is.

One newsman asked him if he thought Oregon hurt him, and it made him laugh. "It certainly wasn't one of the more helpful developments of the day," he said.

It went on like this, just quiet conversation, with everybody just talking around the edges among themselves and with him, and giving the candidate a polite berth. Finally he said, he'd better get to bed, and Dick Tuck—the court jester and advance man—began clearing the small gathering out.

From the first moments when Kennedy learned the bad news aboard his chartered plane returning to Oregon from a day's campaigning in California, his manner was stiff-upper-lippish. Those aboard the plane said he walked down the aisle, smiling, making light conversation, doing what he could to boost the sagging spirits of his closest campaign workers.

To the faithful who met him at the airport and the hordes that jammed

the Benson Hotel lobby when he arrived, he was gracious. A victorylike crush developed in the Benson lobby that threatened to engulf both him and Mrs. Kennedy, who is pregnant, but aides like Bill Barry, experienced at bodyguarding, got them safely to the elevator.

Shortly afterward, when Kennedy appeared in his ballroom election night center for a television appearance, he spoke without visible emotion and without regret. He thanked his workers and praised the people of Oregon, then turned and walked out.

Robert Kennedy in defeat was in ways more magnanimous than in victory. In Nebraska two weeks earlier, he had invited McCarthy supporters to join him, in a gesture that jolted many McCarthyites in its directness. But in Oregon, he took his first electoral defeat—and the first for his family, a family that takes winning and takes family seriously—like a man.

JOSEPH KRAFT
THE LOS ANGELES TIMES
May 30, 1968

They ganged up here in Portland as the returns from the presidency primary came in the other night. But it was not to watch Richard Nixon win the historic victory that practically assures him the Republican nomination and makes him the favorite in the race for President. Neither was it to see the end of the so-called dream ticket—the simultaneous defeat of Governor Ronald Reagan of California and Governor Nelson Rockefeller of New York. Nor did they gather to salute Eugene McCarthy, though the senator from Minnesota won a gallant victory—a victory that makes him big league if anybody is.

No, the main event was watching a Kennedy go down in smoke. They ganged up to tear a passion to tatters—to see Bobby take his lumps. And the question that has to be asked is why it happened, how the Kennedy machine with its infinite resources and ruthless customs let their man go down so visibly and dramatically.

One easy out is to blame the state of Oregon. It is not in any sense representative of the nation, still less of the troubles Kennedy believes himself especially fitted to handle. It has an infinitesimal Negro population. It has almost no white ethnic groups.

It is so much a playground of nature, a patch of mountains and rivers and ocean and desert, that it does not even have city problems. At a Nixon telethon here the other night, thousands of questions came in, and though the respondents were under orders to pick out an urban issue, not one of the questions was about cities. For there really are no urban problems in this state. Indeed, the whole state is a kind of suburb, offering no handles to a Kennedy.

The style of Oregon politics offers another easy out. Traditionally, those who have done well in this state are moralistic loners who fight for lost causes. None of this, of course, is in the Kennedy style. And the senator could well beg off on that score. It could be said that he is a man concerned with the realities of power, who went down to defeat in a state that is against power.

If necessary, it could even be argued that he was overwhelmed. It could be said, and indeed was said by some, that he was defeated not by Senator McCarthy but by the massed might of the Democratic Party Establishment— by money and managerial skill funneled in from Washington for the McCarthy campaign; by the relentless effort waged by labor on behalf of President Johnson and Vice President Humphrey.

But in fact that is nonsense. Neither Hubert Humphrey nor Lyndon Johnson, with their puny vote totals and meager popularity, could have beaten Kennedy in this state. And if it was just a question of avoiding them, he could have ducked the state as Goldwater did when he was confronted with defeat back in 1964.

Still less convincing is the argument that Kennedy will make it all back, and more, in California next week. Maybe he will win California. But the momentum had been interrupted. The spell of victories in Indiana and Nebraska which sent him up in the polls, and thus would have made it hard for Democratic leaders to go against him, has been broken.

So the question abides. Why did he allow himself to take it on the chin so publicly and dramatically when the issue could have been skirted? And the answer has to do with the qualities that people who hate Kennedy can probably never comprehend and that those of us who admire him can probably never communicate.

The answer is that at bottom, no matter what prudence may counsel or advisers whisper, Robert Kennedy is not a man who ducks a challenge or avoids an issue. On the contrary, he has a low anxiety threshold when it comes to taking an uncommitted position.

He sees problems and he meets responsibilities. He is, in the serious sense, an honest man. Which is why he would have been so right as President in a time of troubles, and also why he is now suffering a defeat that will probably deny him the highest office in the land.

EDITORIAL
THE BLACKFOOT NEWS (IDAHO)
June 10, 1968

The concern that Senator Robert F. Kennedy felt for those Americans from whom the American dream seemed most remote was told in the days of mourning that followed his death. Even the cynical among us must be touched by the evidence he indeed achieved a rapport with the objects of his concern.

Soon after his death became known, the thought occurred that it would bring sorrow to some of the people of the Fort Hall Reservation. It remains strong in their minds that in January, 1968, he interrupted a Sun Valley vacation to visit them and conduct a hearing on the reservation for the United States Indian Affairs subcommittee that he headed.

An official expression of their concern may have been sent to Mrs. Ethel Kennedy. It is for these proud and sensitive but muted people to know. But the thought occurred that many individual Indians would feel that when Senator Kennedy died they had lost a friend who cared. Would there be any expression from these people, who in the last three centuries have become undemonstrative in the face of what they may still consider to be hostile power?

The answer may have been found in something that occurred in Blackfoot on Friday.

Early that afternoon an Indian acquaintance who stops occasionally at the office of *The Blackfoot News* came in. He carried with him the smell of liquor. He spoke incoherently.

"He was our friend. Tell them he was our friend. He came to see us."

Almost fiercely he sought a listener. "They should know," he repeated to everyone who would listen. I'm afraid that ears were closed to him. Eventually he wandered out.

About an hour later he returned. This time he confronted this reporter. Tears were streaming down his face.

"I want to tell them that he was our friend. I may be drunk, but I want you to tell them. He came to see us—he talked to my father—he was going to make things better for us. I was a Marine. I fought in many battles for this country. He was the first really big man that came to see us. He saw how we lived. He told us he would help us get new houses. Tell them the Shoshone-Bannock people thought he was their friend. Promise me that you will tell them."

Wiping his tears, the first I ever saw an Indian shed, he reluctantly accepted assurances we would try to get the word to the people who should know. By that time there had emerged a sense of concern for a responsibility placed upon me by another.

Yet a third time the petitioner came back as the afternoon drew to a close. He had regained his composure.

Steadily and with dignity he said:

"I'm not drunk. I'm sorry for acting as if I was before. But he was our friend, and my friends and I want you to tell them." It had not occurred to me that he was acting as a messenger for others too.

Then I remembered a story that came out of World War II that I had read. It seems to me that it was written by Ernie Pyle, but I cannot be sure.

It was a story about the hard-bitten pilots of a group of fighter planes in the Pacific theater of the war. All but one of their group had returned from a mission. Tensely they awaited the report they feared. Eventually it came. Silently they wandered away individually, then reassembled later in a secluded spot. After time passed and bottles had been passed, soft cursing that sounded more like prayers than curses began to emerge as the men found their voices.

This is our effort to tell those who should know that a wake for Senator Robert Kennedy was held Friday in Blackfoot, Idaho, by some men of the Shoshone-Bannock nation.

AMERICAN INDIAN CULTURAL GROUP AT
CALIFORNIA STATE PRISON,
SAN QUENTIN, CALIFORNIA
June 6, 1968

OH GREAT ONE, hear the words of our hearts. I raise my pipe above my head and say: Great Spirit, I pray thee, be good to our dear friend, an unforgettable warrior, Robert F. Kennedy. Toward the great pine trees, north, Cold Wind, treat him kindly. Toward the crest of the rising sun, east, Great Sun, shine on his loved one's lodge each morning. Toward the place where the shadowmaker lives, south, bless this fallen warrior, your son. Toward the land of the setting sun, west, Saying waft on the breezes to our friend, this way. Great Spirit, as you sit in the great council with your warriors, give to your newest, the tranquility of a quiet brook, from the knowledge that his dreams and visions live on. Assure him, Great One, that his deeds will not be forgotten. That his belief was that of your great pipe of peace, and the smoke from that peace pipe goes on. Lowering my pipe of peace, I say, Kind Mother Earth, as you receive our friend to your bosom hold him gently.

Now, Great Spirit, we ask thee let our brother rest, for the journey has been hard. And as he rests, let the howl of the coyote, the soft sounds of a flowing stream, the roar of the bear and the chirping of birds, the wind that whistles and sways the tops of the tall pines, the rustle of leaves as they touch light caresses—let these all be a sweet lullaby, to him that shaketh the hand of his friends, the Indian.

DAVID MURRAY

THE CHICAGO SUN-TIMES
May 1, 1968

At first, there was no joy at all on the faces of the dozen or so five year olds in the tiny, dirty playground at the day nursery.

They stared with wide, solemn eyes through the old cyclone fence topped with drooping barbed wire at Robert F. Kennedy, who had walked a hundred feet down the street Tuesday to see them as they stood in their cage.

Tentatively, they poked their fingers at him through the fence, and he pushed his fingers back at them and there was a smile or two, on both sides. But the children still didn't quite know what to make of this man who was surrounded by all the other people with the cameras and microphones and tape recorders and notebooks.

When he started talking to them, you could hardly hear what he said, it was so soft, and his eyes changed from those of a presidential candidate to something else. And he kept talking and stroking their fingers with his and then one little boy said: "Hey, you're on television, aren't you?" and Kennedy nodded and said yes, he was.

The place was the Day Nursery Association of Indianapolis, and it lies in a grubby section only a few steps away from James Whitecomb Riley's house. Kennedy had gone to the Riley house as part of his campaign for the Presidency.

Outside the Riley house, there had been a bunch of screaming teen-age girls from a nearby parochial school. When a reporter asked some of them why Kennedy turned them on, they couldn't explain except to say he was "so neat," or that he was "just great."

Kennedy turned away from his blue-uniformed idolaters then walked in the bright sunlight to the day nursery and talked for a minute with the women who run it. They said it was mostly for children of broken homes and that the ones here were all five year olds from different parts of the city.

So Kennedy stopped with the children for a minute, and after they got to know him a bit better the man who wants to be president pushed open a gate and went inside and hunkered down and talked to them some more. The television cameras and microphones were there, but that didn't make any difference to the children.

Some of them continued to slide down the sliding board or climb on the Jungle Gym but the others clustered around Kennedy, not saying much, some of them, but just trying to hold on to him.

Two little girls came up and put their heads against his waist and he put

"Sure, I know who you are! You're the nice man named Ruthless Opportunist!"

his hands on their heads. And suddenly it was hard to watch, because he had become in that moment the father they did not know or the elder brother who couldn't talk to them or, more important, listen to them, because most elder brothers and most fathers don't know how to listen to five year olds without thinking about other things.

He had gone to the Riley house because when you are fighting a campaign in Indiana, you have to pay homage to the Hoosier Keats. Before that, there had been a day of talking to union officials and a big walking tour, getting mobbed in this city's Monument Circle. And after that there was going to be another visit to a factory and a reception and all the usual paraphernalia of a big, snazzy, first-cabin presidential primary campaign.

But this hiatus, in front of a gray, American Gothic house with the paint peeling off it, was something else. Gone, for just a moment, was the rhetoric and the playing with audiences and the motorcades and the adulation and the criticism.

The word that came on strongest, as he sat and listened to the children and made a quiet remark now and then, was the word "compassion." This is because—and anyone who has ever dealt with five year olds knows this—you can fool a lot of people in a campaign, and you can create phony issues if you want to, and you can build an image with a lot of sharpsters around you with their computers and their press releases. But lonely little children don't come up and put their heads on your lap unless you mean it.

BONNIE ANGELO
NEWHOUSE NEWSPAPERS
November 1963

His detractors call him ruthless and arrogant. His enthusiasts see him as straightforward and tough.

But the kids whose lives he touches see another side of Attorney General Robert F. Kennedy. He's a friend, a man who comes among them and says, "You matter; we care."

Bob Kennedy's concern for children, all ages, all breeds, is seemingly boundless. Between the multiple pressures of office, he finds time for foreign students, congressional offspring, handicapped youngsters, but time most of all for those who are nobody's children, the legions of forgotten boys and girls who don't even hope for a place in the sun.

Why does he do it? They can't vote, they have no power. The Attorney General's associates say that his work as Chairman of the President's Committee on Juvenile Delinquency relaxes him, gives him an outlet for creative, positive action, a change from a job which is primarily punitive.

Bob Kennedy himself shuns this kind of armchair psychoanalysis. After thinking for a long moment, he had a simple answer. "Basicaliy, I just like young people." He elaborated, picking his words carefully.

"We were fortunate as we were growing up, and a lot of people aren't. I think that we should do something to help them. So much more could be done—young people could do so much more with their lives if extra effort was made to help them help themselves."

To help them, he turns up all over town, doing all kinds of things—throwing out the first ball at a Little League game, fielding tough questions from skeptical foreign students, addressing a 4-H conference, praising the industrious newspaper carriers, inducting new scouts at a rally, dispensing concern and encouragement at a benighted school.

On his way to the airport he may swing by a banquet of the Junior Stonewalls, a group organized by a streetsweeper who spends his free time working with Capital slum boys; on his way home to lunch he may stop his car to talk with high school boys working at part-time jobs made possible by the Attorney General's determination.

But these are surface things. His greater concern is with the basic causes, which are the nation's crucial problems—education, unemployment, civil rights.

One of the Attorney General's first missions after taking office was to visit New York's East Harlem to talk with the kind of kids he is most concerned about.

A member of the Viceroy's gang reported, "He looked like a bop himself, sitting there on the curb, with his coat slung back over his shoulder." The tough Harlem kids found him easy to talk to. "He sounded like he really wanted to do something about it," one marveled. "He spoke nice and had good manners."

When his own brood of eight is summering on Cape Cod, Kennedy turns over the swimming pool of his Virginia estate to underprivileged children, scheduling groups on regular days and furnishing soft drinks for them. This gives him special pleasure.

"Adults forget how much little things, like a chance to go swimming, mean to kids," he explained.

Thousands of other Washington youngsters owe the chance to go swimming to Bob Kennedy. When he learned that two pools in Washington's teeming Negro sections had been closed since 1954 for lack of operating funds, he rounded up the money from Protestant, Catholic, and Jewish groups—and hundreds of children who would have roamed the streets flocked to the pools daily.

The same kind of swift, cut-the-red-tape action resulted when Kennedy, driving through a blighted neighborhood, spotted a vacant lot filled with impounded cars. The next day the police department was busy moving the cars, and a project was launched to convert the lot into a showplace recreation area with such imaginative assets as a surplus jet plane, harbor tug, and army tank.

Professional youthworkers say the Attorney General has a gift for communicating with young people. His direct approach and intense interest, with no pandering, no talking down, can change sullen apathy into enthusiasm.

One recent morning at a predominantly Negro school here, Kennedy spoke sternly to the students, warning them that dropouts jeopardize their futures, urging the students to take responsibilities, "to have respect for your school, your teachers, but mostly for yourselves."

When he asked for questions, a shy silence followed—so instead he asked questions of them. After a few rat-a-tat questions—"How many of you read the front pages? Who's the Governor of Maryland? Who are the Virginia Senators?—a student's hand went up tentatively, and then a flood of questions followed. His answers showed that he understood the financial pressures, the frustrations experienced by the students, old beyond their years.

Finally, pressed for time, he left, cheered and mobbed by eager students as he made his way out of the auditorium. "They will remember today all their lives," said a teacher. "These are forgotten children; it's hard for them to believe that somebody, somebody important, cares."

Aware that education is the key to a better future for these youngsters, Kennedy has been the driving force behind a concerted effort to stop school dropouts. A program of summer jobs was undertaken to give the teen-agers the money to buy bus tokens, lunches, shoes, and through the Attorney General's effort 1100 jobs were turned up, mostly in government agencies.

Handicapped children, in addition to generous financial help from the well-filled Kennedy coffers, get Bob Kennedy's personal attention. At a ceremony promoting a fund drive, he invited a little crippled boy to "come see me, and bring your friends." And so he did—bringing fifteen friends in wheel chairs and braces to the Attorney General's office. There they climbed on the big stuffed tiger, patted the even bigger and live Newfoundland dog Brumus, and talked with the President on the telephone.

Children in need are not the only ones who find a friend in the Attorney General. He is fascinated by foreign students as tomorrow's leaders. Each Christmas he entertains hundreds from all around the world in his cavernous quarters at the Justice Department, and throughout the year meets with smaller groups, giving them tough, fast answers to often hostile questions.

In his Far East good-will trip, he concentrated on students. Heckled at the University of Tokyo, he stood his ground, won his point—and wowed the audience. The hefty profits from his book *Just Friends and Brave Enemies* went to scholarship funds at universities in Tokyo, Indonesia, and West Berlin.

Even the well-cared-for children of government officials have their innings with the President's brother. "In Washington everybody goes to parties, except children," he said one day, and forthwith did something about it. He grilled hamburgers and hotdogs in his office fireplace for the teen-agers, and later brought clowns, puppets, and ponies (borrowed from his own children) into the Justice Department courtyard for the little ones. He picks up the tab, of course, for all the gatherings.

With his unflagging interest in the rising generation, there's a basis of an admirer's summary of his role: "The guy's a lobbyist for kids."

EUGENE PATTERSON
THE ATLANTA CONSTITUTION

The mind returns in grief to glimpses of Robert F. Kennedy that were casual at the time—but now are all that we will see of him. Kennedy, talking quietly to Democratic leaders at the Dinkler Plaza Hotel in 1960, organizing his brother's election victory. Kennedy, talking at the Regency about his own presidential campaign just two months ago, and walking the next day in the King funeral procession.

You could take him or leave him on public issues. But Bobby Kennedy was in private life the kind of man you could only admire, respect, and even love. He was a sensitive and humorous man whom children loved instinctively.

They flocked into the streets and stopped his car at Carrolton when he visited West Georgia College on a hot May day in 1964. It was one of his first public appearances since his brother's assassination. He and Ethel flew into the Carrolton airport in a small army plane. Few adults even came out of the stores to see the maligned Attorney General pass through town, en route to West Georgia College to dedicate the small frame Kennedy chapel there.

But teachers turned some pupils out of classes at an elementary school on the route, and suddenly there was bedlam. Kennedy waded through the adoring small fry grinning as they scrambled to pull at his pants leg for a pat on the head or a handshake. It was love at first sight between them, and the same thing happened with the college-age kids on the West Georgia campus. At a session in the gymnasium they fired questions at him and he fired answers back, saying precisely what he thought about civil rights in 1964. He was visibly startled when his honesty brought him a thunderous ovation from the Georgia youngsters.

He loved to sit among his own brood on the terrace of Hickory Hill on Sunday mornings. They, too, adored him for his quiet, teasing, pseudo-gruff way with them. He attended to their squabbles with a mock-serious gravity that turned anger into helpless laughter.

He was a quiet, gracious man on those Sunday mornings. In such relaxed moments he revealed a depth and dimension his enemies never credited. His airy house was hung with history—with treasured original writings of Jefferson, Adams, Lincoln, Paul Revere. In his study, where he kept the flags that once stood in his brother's Cabinet room, one of the photographs showed two of his children peering from beneath President Kennedy's desk. It was autographed by the late President as follows: "Dear Bobby: They TOLD

ROBERT F. KENNEDY AND EL CORDOBES IN PERU

me you had your people placed throughout the government."

His life seemed to revolve around the young. Older people were the ones who disapproved of him. The young ones sensed his quality.

And it was a great quality. Tough as nails, yes. Ruthless, sometimes; he would not brook incompetence nor would he accept untruth. But he had a high, tempered intelligence and the strength of will to prevail. He also had in his mellower last years a new, easier manner. He began to laugh at himself, to make jokes about his failures.

He also had, always, an impulsive outreach when he was moved—an automatic confession of feeling, an impassioned display of kindness. He believed deeply in the better instincts of man. When he was touched, this well of belief showed itself as his deepest spring.

He thought he could be a good president. And he might have been. Children, whose minds are not yet poisoned by the meanness of life, judged him to be a good man.

JIMMY BRESLIN
THE NEW YORK WORLD JOURNAL TRIBUNE
December 4, 1966

Robert Kennedy's hands fidgeted with the folded sheet of paper he held. On the top of the sheet, in IBM electric typewriting, were the words, "FRANK J. VIOLA, BRONX POSTMASTER." He unfolded the sheet. There was a biography of Viola put into the form of remarks. Kennedy folded the sheet again and stood quietly. Around him, in the gloom of the lobby of the Bronx Main Post Office, the old ones and the young old ones stood in a semicircle.

A man was at a microphone addressing the people. "He'll make you a very, very fine postmaster of which the Bronx can be very proud," the man said.

Frank J. Viola, a carnation in his lapel, stood in the semicircle. His wife, in a bright blue feathered hat and a black cloth coat with a fur collar, stood at one end of the semicircle. Somebody at the microphone said: "I'm going to ask Senator Kennedy, who recommended him along with other congressmen, to say something."

Kennedy stepped up to the lectern and unfolded the sheet of paper. He spoke in a voice that has very little modulation. His hands, red from the cold afternoon, had the hint of nerves in them. "This indication of interest and recognition of ability and talents that Colonel Viola has," he was saying. "... contribution to his country in two wars ... we're grateful to the colonel."

Kennedy stepped back and Viola came up to accept the postmaster's job in the Bronx. Viola made a speech. Kennedy moved to the edge of the semicircle. Mrs. Viola was pushed out into the crowd. Kennedy took her elbow and guided her back and then stepped out to make room for her. She listened to her husband proudly.

It was a very nice ceremony. It was the politics and government jobs and service and parcelling out of power which has always gone on in New York. The ones involved stood in a semicircle and they were all old men. It was not Robert Kennedy's world.

Outside, Kennedy got into the front seat of a white four-door Lincoln convertible. He sat sideways. Bill Barry, a wide-shouldered guy in his late thirty's, was driving. Barry was an FBI agent who always was assigned to Robert Kennedy when Kennedy was the Attorney General. When Kennedy left the job, J. Edgar Hoover, in an expression of his deep feelings for Kennedy, had Barry transferred to Alabama. Barry left the bureau and now is in charge of security for a bank in Manhattan.

Earl Graves, who works in Kennedy's official office in New York, sat in the back. A photographer was next to him. There always is a photographer from someplace sitting in the back of a car Kennedy is in.

Graves took a sheet of paper out of his inside pocket. "SENATOR KENNEDY'S SCHEDULE," the electric typewriting said. Under it was a list of times and places. Graves studied it.

"Lunch, Senator?" he said.

"I'd like a milkshake," Kennedy said. "Can we find a Schrafft's?"

"It's too late now," Barry said. "We're right in the rush hour. Five o'clock already. We're going to have trouble making the next stop as it is."

"Where is the next stop?" Kennedy asked.

"Manhattan and Nassau in Brooklyn," Graves said.

"You won't find a Schrafft's there," Barry said.

"Why Schrafft's?" the photographer said.

"I don't know, I like ice cream," Kennedy said.

His fingers began to drum on the dashboard. He talked about his Newfoundland sheepdog messing the late Senator Harry Byrd's office rug. Barry drove the car across the Triborough Bridge and onto an expressway to Brooklyn. The car came off the expressway and through factory streets and into Greenpoint, which is a place of narrow streets lined by three- and four-story wooden houses which are stained from the soot which hangs in the air.

The car came around a corner and slowed down. A park took up the left side of the block. A commercial street started where the park ended.

"It's right up at the corner," Barry said.

"Well, let's see if we're early first," Kennedy said. "If we are, maybe we can get a milkshake someplace."

Graves got out of the car. He began running, with long steps, toward the corner. Kennedy waited in silence. Graves came loping back. He leaned through the car window.

"We're about fifteen minutes early," he said. "And there's a place right over there—see?—where we can get a milkshake."

Kennedy was looking across the window at the park. The place was McCarren Park, a big stretch of soot-darkened grass and black dirt. Off on the other side, a football team was practicing.

"They're playing football," Kennedy said. "Let's go watch some footfall."

"Don't you want anything?" Graves asked.

Kennedy had the door open and he was sliding onto the sidewalk.

"Bring me some tea over to the football practice," he said.

Barry got out of the car on the other side and walked next to Kennedy. At the low black iron fence, Kennedy did a skip step and hurdled it. On the grass on the other side, he began to trot. His hands were stuck in the pockets of a gray form-fitting topcoat. He trotted across the grass with the photographer running behind him. The camera equipment bag slung over the photographer's shoulder kept bouncing while the photographer tried to keep up.

"AN HONORABLE PROFESSION"

It was five thirty P.M. and the streetlights around the park were on. The team practicing was in white helmets with blue and red stripes. The offensive team was in the huddle, the substitutes standing behind them. The coaches, in baseball caps and raincoats and blue parkas, stood in the crowd behind the huddle. The defensive team waited for the next play to run.

One of the coaches turned around and you could see "St. Francis" printed on the back of the parka.

"This must be St. Francis Prep," somebody behind Kennedy said. "They're about the only school in the city that knows how to play football."

"Good," he said. "I like to see the good ones."

A head looked up from the huddle for a moment. Just the head. The eyes under the helmet looked at this person with his hands in the topcoat pockets and the bleak and bony face and this deliberately cut long hair falling up and down onto the forehead with the motion of his body. The boy in the huddle stood straight up now and looked at Robert Kennedy. The boy's mouth came open. Then his hand automatically reached for the one next to him in the huddle. The other one straightened up and looked around. And now they all looked up and the substitutes began pushing to see who was coming.

It is never any different when Robert Kennedy appears where there are people. There is the glance, the awed look, and the hand reaches for the nearest one to show him, too. Everything stops and then the people are in the street and running toward Kennedy and it always is the young ones who get there first and crowd for his handshake. To tell of this is not to glorify him. There is too much slobbering over him as it is. But to tell it is merely to tell a fact. When they write of Bobby Kennedy as a political force in this country, they write sentences which say, "Bobby's 'new' liberalism actually is more intuitive and pragmatic than it is the expression of conversion to a new set of ideals." Or they write of his old arrogance or new ideas and of his dead brother and his sister-in-law and of his chances in 1968 and 1972. It all comes out as writing done by an adult who has talked to other adults, the old men and the young old men, and the writing is done in an office filled with old men and young old men and the stories probably are important and full of meaning. A lot of smart men are doing the writing. But all of it—all the words about whether Bobby Kennedy is a ruthless, mechanical rich guy or a genius mellowed by great tragedy—all of it is superfluous when you see him coming up to a high school football team that is practicing for a game.

"Never mind me, let's see you run the play," Bobby Kennedy calls out.

The coach steps forward. "All right, let's get back to business," he says.

The heads go down into the huddle. On the defense, a linebacker calls out, "All right, come on, let's do it right. Let's show him how we do it."

With a handclap, the huddle breaks and the team comes out.

"Ready," the quarterback calls out.

"They're very big," Kennedy says.

"Hut one,'" the quarterback says.

"Senator Kennedy, I'm Vince O'Connor, the coach," a guy wearing glasses and a baseball cap says.

"... two ... hut three."

The quarterback starts dropping back and there is a slap as both lines go into each other. The offensive team is running out of a double wing T. The black dirt splits from under the quarterback's feet as he pivots and throws overhand, with good arm extension. The pass is sharp and thrown to the right halfback, who has been spread and came slanting in. The pass is called a look-in pass and the right halfback grabs it in full stride and races past a linebacker.

All the kids let out a yell and clap their hands.

"All right," the coach calls out.

"They're good," Kennedy says. He turns to the coach. "Who are the best ones?"

"We have a tackle, Anthony DiNardo, Senator. He's been all-prep school twice. Ivy League schools want him."

"Which one is he?" Kennedy says.

O'Connor points to two thick legs in the huddle.

"Then we have a halfback who is going to break the all-time city scoring record. Richie Szaro. He's only here three years from Poland."

"Really? Where? Which one is he?"

The team breaks from the huddle. O'Connor points at Szaro. He is the left halfback. He looks about 180 pounds, but with room to grow. The legs tell you that. Strong legs, the long muscle sticking out in a ridge when he gets into his stance. Coal miner's legs. Peasant's legs.

"Hut wan."

"The tackle keeps a high stance," somebody next to Kennedy says.

With a clap of pads, the play is off. The tackle, DiNardo, comes off his stance with a powerful and awfully fast first step, which is almost the whole game when you are a lineman.

"Look at that," Kennedy says. "Gee, he's good." He turns to the coach. "The boy from Poland?"

The coach nods and says something to the quarterback.

Earl Graves comes back, pulling containers out of a bag. He hands Kennedy a container.

The team breaks out of the huddle and O'Connor moves next to Kennedy and points to Szaro.

"He is a left-foot kicker. He played soccer in Poland. We use him for field goals and kickoffs, punts, everything."

They run Szaro on a play that looks like an inside reverse. DiNardo, the big tackle, is plunging ahead, his legs chopping and his arms flailing in a handfight with the defensive man and Szaro has his speed in a step and he comes slapping through the hole, spinning off a hand that grabs him and he flies across the black dirt of the field and runs the play out.

"Terrific," Kennedy says. He keeps his eyes on Szaro. "What are his marks like?"

"He has the potential to go to an Ivy League school, Senator," O'Connor says. "Harvard spoke to us about him."

Kennedy smiles. "Who was it that spoke to you?"

O'Connor mentions a name that is lost in the noise of the kids yelling for the way Szaro had run the play.

"Isn't that wonderful?" Kennedy says to Graves. "Only here three years from Poland and look at how he can play and what he has in front of him. I think that's terrific."

He was sipping the tea. In the huddle you could hear the voices.

"You do it."

"No, you go do it."

"All right, let's go." They break from the huddle and the quarterback runs over. The tea bag had dropped on Kennedy's shoe. The quarterback whisks it up in his hand and throws it away and runs to his position.

They run off more plays and Kennedy yells "two hands" when somebody drops a pass. Or "ooohhh" or "that's the way" when one is completed.

"They can play anybody," he says.

"Schools in Pennsylvania," one with him says.

"Everett," Kennedy says. "Do you know Everett High in Massachusetts?"

"Yes, they're very good," O'Connor, the coach, says.

"These boys here could play Everett anytime," Kennedy says.

It was cold, and it was becoming almost too dark to follow the ball. The kids were running football plays and Kennedy was watching them and rooting for them to run it right. He was excited and eager and they piled into each other because they knew he was watching. They had something between them. The brother, of course. That is always there. And the youth and the long hair and the name and the sister-in-law and just the idea of being young. Whatever it is, it is there for good. Bobby Kennedy can be every inch of the worst s.o.b. we've ever had. Everything he does in public can be a façade. But standing on a football field with kids, nothing matters. There is something between them that is powerful.

Somebody came running across the field waving. "They're ready now," the guy was shouting out.

Kennedy turned and shook hands with the coach and began running across the field to the place he had to be at. The heads came out of the huddle and watched him go.

Later, in his fourteenth floor apartment in the UN Towers, Kennedy sat with his shirt sticking out of his pants and a vodka-on-the-rocks in his hands.

"Weren't they good?" he was saying. "That boy from Poland. I can't get over him. Here only three years and he can play so well. He has all these marvelous things in front of him. Why didn't you stay there with him? I think what he's doing is a lot more interesting than what I'm doing or the Democratic Party is doing or something like that. Only three years

from Poland. Poland! Now he's here. He can have all these things. I think it's terrific."

He turned to Graves, who was standing with a phone to his ear.

"The coach told me they were playing Sunday. See if we can fit the game into the schedule. I want to see the boy play," Kennedy said to Earl Graves.

Graves nodded.

St. Francis Prep played against Chaminade High School on Sunday at a place called Boys' High Field, which is in Brooklyn. Richie Szaro kicked a forty-five-yard field goal and then was seen running that play which seems to be an inside reverse. He slammed through, was hit squarely by a linebacker and immediately spun and came into another one leading with his side, not his whole body, and those peasant legs kept kicking and trying to get into rhythm and suddenly they were all motion and he was free of hands and he raced nine yards into the end zone. He is going to be a big football player at a college in a couple of years.

Bobby Kennedy did not make the game. At one point in his schedule that Sunday he started to ask about it and they told him it would take forty-five minutes to get to the field and they didn't have the time. So he said all right and, immersed in work, forgot about it.

When the game was over on Sunday, the St. Francis kids crowded into a narrow locker room that had a low cement ceiling. They had won easily. The kids grabbed the doors of the green metal lockers and began to bang in rhythm.

"We're number one," they chanted.

They stopped chanting and broke into a cheer when O'Connor, the coach, walked in. O'Connor was holding the game ball over his head.

"Senator Kennedy," the kids yelled. "The ball goes to Senator Kennedy."

They yelled it loud. Young faces, streaked with mud from a game, young faces of boys sixteen and seventeen and eighteen. The same young faces that are all over the country and they don't want to know anything about old men or young old men. The only name they know in politics is Robert Kennedy, the president's brother. Young faces, and some of them will be twenty-one in 1968 and all of them will be twenty-one in 1972 and this is not a story about politics, it is a story about simple arithmetic.

MRS. JOSEPH P. KENNEDY
STATEMENT TO AMERICAN PEOPLE

"May I extend my sincere thanks to all you dear friends who offered your prayers, affection, and condolences at the time of our recent bereavement.

"We know that these tributes came straight from your heart and our hearts responded with gratitude and deep appreciation. We cannot always understand the ways of almighty God—the crosses which He sends us, the sacrifices which He demands of us—but we believe in His divine goodness, in His wisdom.

"We accept with faith and resignation His holy will with no looking back to what might have been, and we are at peace. We have courage for the future, and we shall carry out the principles for which Bobby stood.

"His devotion, his dedication to those high ideals, are well known, and we shall honor him not with useless mourning and vain regrets for the past, but with firm and indomitable resolutions for the future—acting now to relieve the starvation of people in this country, working now to aid the disadvantaged and those helpless, inarticulate masses for whom he felt so deeply and for whom he worked long hours, night as well as day.

"And in our thoughts of him and in our prayers, we shall remember Ethel as well as his little children with whom he laughed and prayed that they, too, may remember their father not as only a parent who gaily shared their sports and their childhood triumphs, but also as one who pledged his heart, soul and strength to the betterment of humanity and the enrichment and honor of our great country, the United States of America."

SENATOR EDWARD M. KENNEDY
STATEMENT TO AMERICAN PEOPLE

"I hope that the countless thousands who have sent their expressions of sympathy and condolence to Ethel Kennedy and my mother and father and members of the Kennedy family can realize the strength and the hope that they have given to the members of the family during these last several days.

"This has not been the first tragedy that has afflicted my parents and the members of my family, and we pray that it is the last. But in each instance, in spite of a world of cruelty, we have been much more impressed with the compassion and the love and the warmth of the human heart than we have over any other emotion.

"We are deeply indebted to President and Mrs. Johnson for their words as well as their actions, to the Vice President of the United States for his assistance, and we have been consoled by His Holiness Pope Paul, the Secretary General of the United Nations and other heads of state and many political leaders.

"But most of all, it has been the people, the people themselves, with outstretched hands of sympathy and strength that have most touched the hearts of the members of my family. It is the ones who could give the least who have given the most. To those who have expressed their grief and who have raised their voices to the members of our family, we shall always be deeply grateful.

"To the thousands who filed through St. Patrick's and stood on the streets of New York and stood on that railroad embankment, the other thousands who stood in the rain in Washington, D.C., to those in California, the longshoremen who paused for a few minutes in their work, to the graduates and commencement speakers in the Midwest, to those who offered prayers on the battleship *Massachusetts* in my own state of Massachusetts in Fall River, we shall never be able to express adequately in words our thanks but we shall in our deeds, in our public and private lives.

"And to those who began the campaign and carried on the campaign for the ideals for which Robert Kennedy believed, that dream still remains, and those hopes still remain.

"And each of us will have to decide in a private way, in our own hearts, and in our consciences, what we shall do in the course of this summer, and in future summers, and I know we shall choose wisely.

"Ethel and the members of the family are doing well. They have returned to school. Their oldest daughter Kathleen is teaching in an Indian reservation this summertime. They have the strength that their father has given them, and we pray to God that the Lord will give them the health to carry on."